A WORLD BANK STUDY

An Operational Framework for Managing Fiscal Commitments from Public-Private Partnerships

The Case of Ghana

Riham Shendy
Helen Martin
Peter Mousley

THE WORLD BANK
Washington, D.C.

Contents

Acknowledgments

This report was developed by the Financial and Private Sector Development Department, Africa Region (AFTFP). The authoring team comprised Riham Shendy, Helen Martin, and Peter Mousley. The study was produced at the request of the Government of Ghana (GoG) under the leadership of the Public Investment Division (PID) of the Ministry of Finance and Economic Planning (MoFEP) and with support from DFID.

The authoring team wishes to thank World Bank colleagues for their valuable input, including Dante Mossi, Lincoln Flor, Clive Harris, Lars Jessen, Rui Monteiro, Alan Moody, Sophie Sirtaine, and Eriko Togo. The team is also grateful to IMF colleagues for feedback provided by Benedict Clements, Timothy Irwin, Florence Kuteesa, and Genevieve Verdier. Additional thanks to the Ghana DFID team: Tom Crowards, Ruby Bentsi, and Abena Sono for their support. Finally, appreciation is given to manager Paul Noumba Um for the guidance he provided in the drafting of the report.

In May 2012 and September 2012, the content of this study was discussed and presented to the various stakeholders in MoFEP, namely PID, Debt Management Division, Budget Division, External Economics Relations Division, and the Economic Research and Forecasting Division. The team wishes to thank all government counterparts for their valuable input.

Acronyms

AICD	Africa Infrastructure Country Diagnostic
BD	Budget Division (of MoFEP)
CA	Contracting Authority
CBA	Cost-Benefit Analysis
CL	Contingent Liabilities
DMD	Debt Management Division (of MoFEP)
DMO	Debt Management Office
DSA	Debt Sustainability Analysis
EPCC	Economic Policy Coordinating Committee
ERFD	Economic Research and Forecasting Division
ERG	Exchange Rate Guarantee
EU	European Union
FC	Fiscal Commitments
FCTC	Fiscal Commitment Technical Committee
FS	Feasibility Study
GDP	Gross domestic product
GFSM	Government Finance Statistics Manual
GHC	Ghanaian Cedi
GIFMIS	Ghana Integrated Financial Management Information System
GoG	Government of Ghana
GWCL	Ghana Water Company Limited
IFRS	International Financial Reporting Standards
IMF	International Monetary Fund
IPP	Independent Power Producer
IPSAS	International Public Sector Accounting Standards
MCA	Multi-Criteria Analysis
MDA	Ministries, Departments and Agencies
MMDAs	Metropolitan, Municipal and District Assemblies

MoFEP	Ministry of Finance and Economic Planning
MRG	Minimum Revenue Guarantee
MTDS	Medium Term Debt Management Strategy
MTEF	Medium Term Expenditure Framework
NIP	National Infrastructure Plan
NPV	Net Present Value
OECD	Organisation for Economic Co-operation and Development
PAU	Project Advisory Unit (of PID)
PFA	Project and Financial Analysis Unit (of PID)
PFI	Private Finance Initiative
PFS	Pre-Feasibility Study
PID	Public Investment Division (of MoFEP)
PIP	Public Investment Plan
PPA	Power Purchasing Agreement
PPP	Public-Private Partnership
PPP AC	Public-Private Partnership Approval Committee
PRMA	Petroleum Revenue Management Act
PV	Present Value
SEC	State Enterprise Commission
SOE	State-Owned Enterprise
SPV	Special Purpose Vehicle
TA	Transaction Advisor
TC	Technical Committee
TMU	Technical Memorandum of Understanding
TOR	Terms of Reference
VfM	Value for Money
VGF	Viability Gap Fund
VRA	Volta River Authority

CHAPTER 1

Introduction

The "National Policy on PPP" recently approved by the Government of Ghana (GoG) sets out the government's intention to use Public-Private Partnerships (PPPs) to "improve the quality, cost-effectiveness, and timely provision of public infrastructure in Ghana." In June 2011, the Cabinet approved the National Policy on PPPs (referred to as the "PPP Policy" hereafter), which sets out the principles that will guide the implementation of PPPs in Ghana. As defined in the PPP Policy, a PPP is a "contractual arrangement between a public entity and a private sector party, with clear agreement on shared objectives for the provision of public infrastructure and services traditionally provided by the public sector."[1]

PPPs can help address a part of the huge infrastructure gap that cannot be financed from the public purse. The Ghana "Africa Infrastructure Country Diagnostic" Report AICD (2010) estimates that raising the country's infrastructure endowment to that of the Sub-Saharan Africa region's middle-income countries requires addressing both efficiency and a funding gap of US$1.5 billion per annum, highlighting the potential role of private sector participation. Not addressing the gap has a high opportunity cost that could significantly impact the country's growth and development. Building the required infrastructure through PPPs is one option to address the infrastructure needs given the country's present budgetary fiscal constraints. However, if clear arrangements for undertaking PPPs are not established with caution, they are likely to constitute a burden on the government and to erode efficiency benefits associated with PPPs.

The PPP Policy highlights the role of the government's financial support to PPPs, as well as the importance of putting in place a system to manage the associated fiscal commitments (FCs). As noted in the policy, the government's contribution to a PPP may include remuneration to the private party from government budgets, which "may be fixed or partially fixed, periodic payments (annuities) and contingent."[2] Managing these kinds of long-term and uncertain payment commitments can be challenging, and the government is at risk of building up significant fiscal exposure. For this reason, Paragraph 19 of the PPP Policy states that the institutional arrangements established for the successful implementation of PPP program will include "the institutional framework to support the function of financial management of funded and contingent obligations from PPPs."

This report proposes an operational framework for managing fiscal obligations arising from PPPs in Ghana. This framework aims to ensure that PPP FCs are consistently identified and assessed during PPP project preparation, and that these assessments are fed into project approval. The framework will also ensure that PPP FCs are monitored, reported on, and budgeted for appropriately over the lifetime of PPP projects. To that end, the report outlines roles and responsibilities, concepts, and processes for managing PPP FCs, drawing on international standards and practices, bearing in mind existing institutions and capacities in Ghana. The report also suggests legislative additions and capacity building needed to establish this framework in practice.

Most of the recommendations in this report can be immediately applied by the GoG. Others may be implemented in the future, as the PPP program expands or when Ghana adopts updated accounting approaches (such as full accrual International Public Sector Accounting Standards [IPSAS]). In light of the recommendations in the report, appendix A summarizes the decisions and actions that GoG can take in the short term to tackle this topic. For each activity outlined in appendix A, the rationale and justifications are provided in the main text of the report. Appendix A also includes a list of projects for which the GoG could initiate a PPP FC stocktaking exercise, in line with the recommendations outlined in this report.

This report focuses primarily on managing long-term FCs to PPPs, including regular payments or contingent liabilities (CL) that typically last throughout a project's lifetime. These types of commitments are challenging to manage, given their long-term horizon—beyond the typical planning and budgeting framework of the government. They are also likely to be relevant to a number of PPP deals currently being developed in Ghana, such as the Asutsuare Water Treatment project, which will involve annual payments for the bulk water by Ghana Water Company Ltd (GWCL); several Independent Power Producers (IPPs) that also create annual payment obligations for the Volta River Authority (VRA) through the Power Purchase Agreements; and the Korele Bu Diagnostic/Imaging Lab, which is likely to entail regular service payments by the Ministry of Health.

The Government may also provide upfront transfers to PPPs to finance construction. This type of support extends over a shorter-time horizon—typically the construction period, which may last up to three or four years. Since this type of support takes place over the same time horizon as a typical public sector investment, it is more straightforward to manage through the usual public financial management systems. Moreover, the GoG is currently considering options for introducing a "Viability Gap Funding" system that would be specifically geared toward managing GoG capital contributions to PPP projects.

This report is structured as follows. Chapter 2 introduces the concept of FCs from PPPs: how and why PPPs create FCs, why managing them is important, and an overview of what it entails. Chapters 3 to 5 present the framework proposed for Ghana for managing FCs from PPPs. Chapter 3 presents institutional roles and responsibilities; chapter 4 describes how FC management should be incorporated in the PPP development and approval process; and chapter 5 describes how FCs can be managed during PPP implementation by monitoring, reporting, and budgeting adequately. Chapter 6 sets out the steps needed to begin to implement this PPP framework—to build its core requirements into the forthcoming PPP Law, and to build capacity in the relevant entities to carry out those requirements in practice.

Notes

1. The report is based on meetings with the relevant divisions in MoFEP. The framework presented draws heavily and builds on: Irwin (2009), Cebotari (2008), and the World Bank Institute's PPP Reference Guide Version 1.0 (WBI 2012).

2. National PPP Policy, Paragraph 7.

CHAPTER 2

Managing Fiscal Commitments to PPPs: What and Why?

Public-private partnerships (PPPs) can bring private sector finance, experience, and efficiency to bear in providing quality infrastructure services at better value for money than traditional government procurement. The government's contribution to the "partnership" of PPP, however, often gives rise to fiscal commitments (FCs) throughout the lifetime of the project. Unless these commitments are managed well, the potential advantages of PPP can be eroded, and the government can risk building up significant fiscal exposure. This chapter sets out why and how PPPs create FCs, why managing those commitments is important, and what it entails.

How and Why PPPs Create FCs

Using PPPs to develop infrastructure can bring two principal benefits: a new source of financing and the potential for efficiency gains. By involving private sector investment, public funding requirements for infrastructure can be spread over a longer-time horizon. This enables faster expansion of infrastructure services for a given "fiscal space," although the total resources available for infrastructure over the longer term are unchanged—that is, under a PPP, the government saves in investment outlays but relinquishes future potential revenue from fees (where the PPP is paid for with user fees) or other uses of future tax revenues (if the PPP company is paid by the government).[1] The second benefit of PPPs arises from efficiency gains associated with private sector participation. These efficiency gains are primarily achieved through bundling the financing, design, construction, operation, and maintenance of infrastructure, rather than the involvement of private finance per se—for example, by providing stronger incentives to adopt a design that is cost-effective over the infrastructure's lifetime and to complete construction on time and on budget.[2]

The government's contribution to the "partnership" of a PPP often creates FCs. Under a well-structured PPP, the government almost always bears some risk or provides some financial support. These government contributions are

5

needed to mobilize private investment in a way that provides value for money for two broad reasons:

- **To subsidize or pay for viable projects**—where economically viable projects are not financially viable through user charges alone, or where user charging is not desirable or practical, governments may provide subsidies to enable the private party to earn an adequate return on investment. Ongoing subsidies—for example, annual payments over the lifetime of a toll road conditional on its availability at a specified quality, or output-based subsidy payments per kilometer driven—are alternatives to up-front capital or in-kind subsidies.
- **To achieve an appropriate risk allocation**—one of the key ways that a PPP can achieve value for money (VfM) compared to traditional government procurement is by ensuring that each party bears the project risks they are best able to manage efficiently. Allocating too much risk to the private party may make it expensive or impossible to raise finance. This means that under a well-structured PPP, the government is likely to bear or share some project risks—for example, this could include guaranteeing a certain level of traffic for a toll road PPP, or in some cases, sharing overall risk by providing a credit-enhancing guarantee.

The impact of the global financial crisis on the PPP market has increased the need for government support to enable PPP deals to close. This has often involved governments bearing more risk under PPPs, as described in box 2.1.

The FCs that the government accepts under a PPP can be either direct or contingent. "Direct" liabilities are those where the need for payment is known—these could include an up-front capital payment or regular payments (such as availability payments) over the lifetime of the contract. "Contingent" liabilities (CL) are those for which payment is needed only if some uncertain future event or circumstance occurs—so the occurrence, value, and timing of a payment may all be unknown. Table 2.1 provides examples of both types of liabilities. These liabilities are created by clauses in the PPP contractual agreements—that is, they are explicit liabilities.[3] PPPs may also create implicit liabilities for the government—that is, obligations that are not legally binding—typically because of the government's implicit obligation to ensure continuous provision of basic public services. However, one of the aims of writing a good PPP contract is to make risk allocation, and hence liabilities, as explicit as possible. This report therefore focuses for the most part on managing explicit FCs to PPPs.

PPPs undertaken by State-Owned Enterprises (SOEs) also create CLs for the government. Where SOEs such as Ghana Water Company Limited (GWCL) or Volta River Authority (VRA) enter into PPP agreements, those contracts may create financial commitments for the SOE of any of the types described in table 2.1. This in turn typically creates FCs for the government. This may be because of explicit government guarantees on the payment

Box 2.1

Impact of the Global Financial Crisis on the PPP Market and Government Responses

There are several channels through which the financial crisis affected the public-private partnership (PPP) market. The financial sector suffered reduced liquidity, scarce regulatory capital, upward pressure on interest rates, and a collapse in the wrapped bond market due to the downfall of the mono-line insurers (which previously guaranteed project bonds to achieve an investment grade rating). Additionally the crisis has affected the perceptions of risks by the various PPP parties and the private sector risk-return trade-off (such as for unforeseen exchange rate movements). Furthermore, there is the real effect of the economic downturn on project revenue cash flow through the reduced demand for services (for example, lower revenues from landing fees in airports and lower toll road revenues) and the limited ability of private partners to cope with higher costs by passing them on to service users.

In this context, many governments have found that new forms of support are needed—under which the government bears more risk—to enable PPP deals to close. A recent note on the European Union (EU) PPP market outlines two main avenues being explored by several countries after the crisis: sovereign guarantees applied to project debt or project bonds, and co-lending by the government. Examples of recent developments include: sharing interest rate risk in Korea; loan guarantee facilities in France and Portugal; and facilities for direct loans to PPPs in France and the United Kingdom.[a]

a. In Burger et al. (2009) and EPEC (2009).

obligations of the SOE under the project. Alternatively, it may be because of the government's implicit commitment to continuous operation of the SOE, given the importance of the service provided—which may lead to fiscal transfers should the SOE become financially unsustainable for any reason, including its obligations under a PPP contract.

Management of PPP FCs in Ghana will therefore intersect with effective governance of SOEs. This requires that the Ministry of Finance and Economic Planning (MoFEP) oversees the use of PPPs throughout the public sector—including those undertaken by SOEs. For the latter, analysis of fiscal costs and risks should include assessing the financial health of those entities and their ability to meet their contractual commitments.[4] In this context, three key questions need to be considered: (1) how the proposed approval process for PPPs relates to the existing governance of SOEs; (2) how the proposed monitoring fits alongside existing monitoring of SOEs; and (3) how SOEs report their commitments to PPPs (such as what accounting standards are followed, and the extent to which SOEs are included in the financial reporting for the government as a whole). Some of these issues will be addressed in the chapters that follow.

Table 2.1 Types of FCs in PPP Projects

Fiscal commitment	Description
	Direct fiscal commitments
Up front[a]	
Up-front viability payment	The government provides an up-front capital subsidy to the PPP contractor (which may be phased over construction or against equity investments, but only over the first years—that is, the construction phase—of the project lifetime).
Associated works	The government undertakes works that will contribute to the project, such as feeder roads (for a toll road) or dredging (for a port)—again, this type of support typically does not give rise to an ongoing commitment.
Ongoing	
Annuity or availability payments	The government provides a fixed, ongoing subsidy, paid (typically annually) over the lifetime of the project, and often not starting until the construction phase is complete. This payment may be conditional on the availability of the service or asset at a contractually specified quality (called an availability payment[b]). The value of the payments is usually a key financial bid criterion in the tender process to select the private contractor.
Shadow tolls or output-based subsidies	The government provides a subsidy per unit or user of a service—for example, per kilometer driven on a toll road. Again, the unit value of such a subsidy would typically be the financial bid criterion.
	Contingent liabilities
"Guarantees" on particular risk variables	The government commits to compensate the private party for loss in revenue should a particular risk variable deviate from a contractually specified level. The associated risk is thereby shared between the government and the private party. For example, this could include guarantees on the following: · Demand remaining above a specified level, or within a specified range · Exchange rates remaining within a specified range · Tariffs being allowed to follow a specified formula (where tariffs are set or approved by a government entity)
Force majeure compensation clauses	The government commits to compensate the private party for damage or loss due to certain specified *force majeure* events. These are typically limited to those events for which insurance is not commercially available, which may include certain natural disasters.
Termination payment commitments	The government commits to pay an agreed amount should the contract be terminated due to default either by the private party or by the government on their obligations under the contract, and to take control of the project assets. Typically, the defined payment is lower in case of private party default.
Credit guarantees	The government guarantees repayment of some or all of the debt taken on by the project company if the project company itself defaults on the debt, regardless of the reason for the default.

Source: World Bank and Castalia 2011.
Note: PPP = public-private partnership.
a. This report focuses on managing ongoing fiscal commitments (FCs). Up-front commitments are included here for completeness.
b. Although conditional on availability, this is considered a direct liability because, provided both parties comply with the contract, it will need to be paid (unlike the contingent liabilities [CLs] described thereafter).

Challenge of Managing PPP FCs—Why a Framework Is Needed

Managing FCs under PPPs poses several challenges. Most of the FCs previously described are long term—extending over the lifetime of the PPP contract—and often do not start until several years after contract signing. Payments for CLs are by definition uncertain, and in some cases can arise suddenly and unexpectedly. By contrast, Government of Ghana (GoG) budgets on a cash basis,[5] with a relatively short planning horizon (for example, the three-year Medium Term Expenditure Framework, or MTEF), and follows a process designed to be relatively inflexible to "in-year" changes. In this environment, managing ongoing FCs typically poses four key challenges:

- Long-term or contingent commitments are often not subject to the usual affordability checks on government expenditures provided by the annual budget or medium-term planning processes (such as the MTEF), since payments occur outside the budget and planning horizon. This means decision makers may not fully take into account the cost to government of such commitments.
- Risks associated with CLs for the government need to be proactively managed over the lifetime of the project to achieve VfM.
- Uncertain payment obligations expose the government to fiscal risk that can create budgetary uncertainty and may put the public debt on an unsustainable path.
- Uncertainty among private partners as to whether the government will be able to honor its commitments promptly can undermine the VfM created by allocating risks well.

Because of these challenges, governments can also be tempted to undertake PPPs for the "wrong" reasons. If FCs are not clearly acknowledged and managed, PPPs may be pursued simply to postpone the budget impact of public investment, and to move the associated debt off the government "balance sheet, in a way that does not take into account the longer-term implications for public finances. This can undermine the possible advantages of PPPs, and increase the risk of building up significant fiscal exposure in the future.

Historical experiences have demonstrated the importance of managing government fiscal support to PPPs. In the midst of the 1997 Asian crisis, several Asian countries suffered exacerbated impacts due to PPP CLs that transformed into immediate obligations. While the banking sector was the major source of fiscal liabilities in Korea, infrastructure projects added to the fiscal stress. In Indonesia, concerns have been raised regarding the role of the Ministry of Finance, which had the chance to intervene in the development of a concession only when it was too late to propose major changes without serious disruption to the investment program. This led to messy government responses to claims of compensation by investors in the wake of the 1997 crisis, which ultimately crippled many of the projects. Such problems may have been more effectively addressed if the Ministry of Finance had assessed the fiscal obligations of these deals at approval.[6]

More recently, under the current financial and economic crisis, a number of European countries have faced the reality of the fiscal implications of their PPP projects. Portugal and Hungary have placed a moratorium on new PPPs and are reviewing existing ones. Portugal's recent crisis has been exacerbated by the fact that the government currently has to make large payments to PPP companies as a result of PPP contracts developed in the years before the crisis without adequate consideration of their fiscal implications. Additionally, the United Kingdom slashed its "Building Schools for the Future" PPP program and is now reviewing its PPP policy (known in the United Kingdom as the "Private Finance Initiative," or PFI).[7]

Several countries have run successful PPP programs for some time without comprehensive frameworks specifically geared to managing the associated FCs. For instance Chile, whose concession program started in 1992, began to explicitly address this concern in 2001/02, when it requested World Bank advice on refining public management systems and improving decision making for guarantees to road PPPs. To date, neither the Republic of Korea nor India[8] has a clear framework for managing all types of fiscal support to PPPs including CLs. In many cases, elements of PPP FC management are built into broader public financial management systems, but they are not presented as a specific framework.[9]

Given the nascent PPP market in Ghana, the framework presented in this report aims to ensure basic management of FCs, without stifling development of PPP projects. It will be some time before the Ghanaian PPP program will build up significant fiscal exposure—particularly in comparison with other common types of government obligations and CLs, such as implicit obligations to SOEs or the banking sector, or pension obligations. The framework outlined in this study is therefore not intended to create undue constraints on the development of a PPP market at this early stage. The purpose is simply to build into the PPP Policy and institutional framework a system that ensures awareness, transparency, and appropriate mitigation of the risks and costs incurred in PPP projects that commit resources of current and future administrations.

Components of a PPP FC Management Framework

As described above, the objectives of the FC management framework set out in this report are to ensure awareness and transparency of the government's FCs under PPP projects and to mitigate the associated fiscal risk. This requires careful consideration of the fiscal implications of a PPP before entering into a PPP contract, and appropriate management of those fiscal implications over the contract lifetime, at both a project and portfolio level.

To this end, there are three key components to the FC management framework set out in this report. The various subcomponents, illustrated in figure 2.1 and described in turn in the chapters that follow, comprise:

- Defining clear roles and responsibilities for managing FCs for PPPs throughout the project cycle
- Building the requirement to assess and approve FCs into the PPP development and approval process set out in the PPP Policy ("PPP development stage")
- Ensuring FCs are adequately managed during PPP project implementation—by monitoring FCs at a project and portfolio level; reporting on and disclosing them as part of regular government financial reporting; and budgeting for them as needed ("PPP implementation stage").

These elements are interlinked—for example, setting out clear requirements for disclosing and budgeting for commitments to PPPs helps ensure discipline when assessing them in the first place. The FC framework is likely to be formalized through a combination of stipulations in PPP legislation, guidance material, and templates or reporting standards.

Figure 2.1 Overview of a FC Management Framework for PPPs[a]

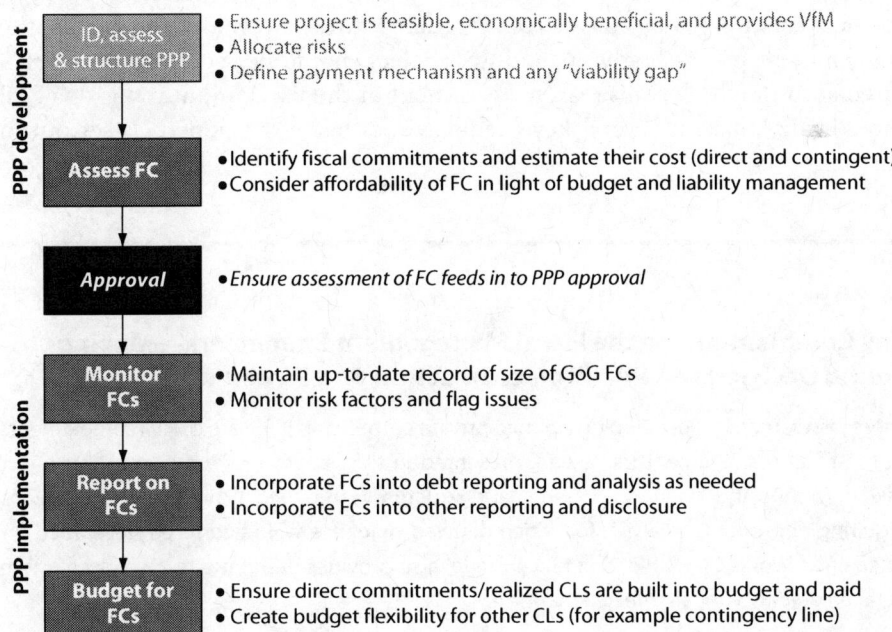

Source: World Bank data.
Note: CLs = contingent liabilities; FCs = fiscal commitments; GoG = Government of Ghana; PPP = public-private partnership; VfM = value for money.
a. While the first component is critical in the public-private partnership (PPP) development process, as described in this chapter, these elements are beyond the scope of this report.

This approach to managing FCs for PPPs is a part of the broader PPP policy, legal, and institutional framework currently being developed by the GoG, centered on the PPP Policy. Several other elements of the PPP framework will be crucial complements to the system set out in this report. As illustrated in figure 2.1, this includes in particular the "upstream" processes of identifying, assessing, and structuring a potential PPP.

Upstream decisions on PPP design and selection are some of the most important determinants of the fiscal implications of a PPP. If the underlying project does not make sense, or if the PPP is not structured in a way that will achieve VfM, then a PPP cannot be fiscally responsible, even if its cost is well understood and managed. It is suggested that the post-Asian crisis realization of the CL largely resulted from inadequate project design and poor investment decisions.[10] These decisions—choosing a particular project; deciding to do that project as a PPP; and deciding how that PPP is structured (including allocating risks and responsibilities and defining payment mechanisms)—are also central elements of the PPP development process. Principles to guide these decisions are already set out in the PPP Policy, as described in box 2.2. Detailed guidance materials, such as risk allocation matrices, are expected to be developed over time.

This report focuses on the "downstream" assessment and management of the fiscal implications of a PPP. For the purposes of this report, the structure of a proposed PPP is assumed to have been developed following the requirements of the PPP Policy. In practice, this is an iterative process—if a certain PPP project or structure is not considered affordable, this view should feed into the development process early on, and the project should be redefined or restructured accordingly. For this reason, assessment of the fiscal implications of a PPP should take place at several key points as it is being developed, as set out in chapter 4.

Box 2.2

Key Complements to the Fiscal Management Framework—Making Sound Decisions on PPP Project Selection and Structuring

Three key elements of developing a public-private partnership (PPP) are crucial complements to the fiscal management framework presented in this report: the approaches to project selection; choosing when to use a PPP; and structuring that PPP. All are complex decisions requiring appropriate analysis, for which detailed guidance will need to be developed for Ghana. The World Bank's PPP Reference Guide[a] also provides descriptions and links to more detailed guidance for all three elements.

Choosing a Good Project—Project Appraisal and Economic Analysis: All public infrastructure projects—whether PPPs or traditional public investments—should be based on

(box continues on next page)

Box 2.2 Key Complements to the Fiscal Management Framework—Making Sound Decisions on PPP Project Selection and Structuring *(continued)*

thorough project appraisal to ensure the project represents a good use of public funds. In some sectors, this may involve long-term planning processes involving analysis across multiple criteria. Such appraisal would typically include considering whether a project is in line with government strategic priorities; feasible (technically, legally, socially, and environmentally); and socioeconomically beneficial—for example, through Cost-Benefit Analysis (CBA) or Multi-Criteria Analysis (MCA).

This kind of analysis can help the following: assess whether or not a project should be undertaken at all; assess different options, such as the timing and scale of an investment; and consider the relative priority of different projects. For example, for a highway investment a government may use CBA or MCA to determine the best timing of road expansion and the appropriate number of lanes, given information on traffic data and alternative transport developments, as well as consider the relative benefits of investing in other transport improvements. CBA builds on financial analysis of the costs and benefits of a project, but adjusts to capture nonfinancial elements (such as externalities, or a preference for use of local labor and resources), and is neutral to the source and structure of financing for a project.

Choosing When to Use PPP—Value for Money Assessment: As the PPP Policy states, "value for money is the driver for adopting the PPP approach." That is, the key determinant in deciding whether to implement a project as a PPP or through traditional public investment will be an assessment of whether a PPP will provide better value for money (VfM). VfM may be achieved through multiple drivers such as: risk transfer, whole of life costing, output specifications, competition, performance measurement, and private sector management skills. Assessing the VfM of a proposed PPP can include a qualitative assessment of whether these factors are likely to apply. It can also include a quantitative assessment of the overall project costs (and in some cases benefits) compared to the alternative of traditional public procurement, taking into account, for example, the different allocation of risks and likely efficiency impacts.

Structuring the PPP Well—Allocating Risks and Responsibilities: Appropriate risk allocation is a key element of achieving VfM from a PPP. The PPP Policy establishes a clear principle for risk allocation: risks should be allocated to the party best able to control and manage them in such a manner that value for money is maximized. In practice, this means that the government will typically bear some risk under a well-structured PPP project, giving rise to fiscal exposure. For example, in a toll road this might involve providing a guarantee of a minimum level of traffic—on the basis that the risk of lower-than-expected traffic should be shared between the private party and government, since it can only be partly controlled by either party (such as, on the government's side, through its control of other transport options). The decision of which risks the government should bear is outside the scope of this report, which focuses on understanding the fiscal implications of the PPP structure. In practice, the process may be iterative, as assessment of the fiscal implications may feed back into a revision of a proposed PPP risk allocation.

(box continues on next page)

Box 2.2 Key Complements to the Fiscal Management Framework—Making Sound Decisions on PPP Project Selection and Structuring *(continued)*

A related element of PPP structuring is defining the payment mechanism that enables private sector cost recovery. This could include defining sector tariff policies that allow for tariff adjustment mechanisms, through government payments in the form of ongoing or up-front capital support, or through a combination of the two. The decision of the structure of government financial support to a PPP is closely interrelated with risk allocation, since different types of support allocate certain key risks (such as demand) differently. Irwin (2003) sets out a framework intended to help governments make good decisions about when to provide and how to structure financial support to infrastructure projects. This report, in contrast, focuses on understanding and managing the fiscal implications of providing that support.

a. WBI 2012.

Notes

1. EIB (2010).
2. WBI PPP Reference Guide (2012), Chapter 1.1.
3. See Polackova Brixi (1998, 2002) for more information on the typology of fiscal liabilities: direct, contingent, explicit, or implicit.
4. Recommendation of the Council on Principles for Public Governance of Public-Private Partnerships, http://acts.oecd.org/Instruments/ShowInstrumentView.aspx?InstrumentID=275&InstrumentPID=281&Lang=en&Book=Fals.
5. This Government of Ghana (GoG) accounting method commonly used by government agencies combines accrual-basis accounting with cash-basis accounting. Modified accrual accounting recognizes revenues when they become available and measurable and, with a few exceptions, recognizes expenditures when liabilities are incurred. This system divides available funds into separate entities within the organization to ensure that the funds are being spent where they were intended.
6. Irwin and Mokdad (2009) and Wells and Ahmed (2006).
7. http://bankwatch.org/public-private-partnerships/background-on-ppps/build-now-pay-heavily-later; and Abrantes, de Sousa, and Lusofonia (2011).
8. In India, clear guidelines exist for the use of the Viability Gap Fund (VGF) instrument, and an Inter-Ministerial Task Force was recently created to recommend budgetary ceilings for annuity commitments under public-private partnership (PPP) projects. Contingent liability (CL) management and monitoring and disclosure of ongoing PPP FCs have not been specifically addressed to date.
9. Irwin and Mokdad (2009) set out the approaches of Chile, South Africa, and Australia for managing Contingent liabilities (CLs) under public-private partnership (PPP) projects.
10. Polackova Brixi (1998, 2002).

CHAPTER 3

Institutional Roles and Responsibilities for Managing PPP FCs

The Public-Private Partnership (PPP) Policy establishes the general institutional framework for managing PPPs, including roles and responsibilities that are relevant to managing fiscal commitments (FCs) from PPP projects. This chapter first summarizes these roles and responsibilities as currently defined in the PPP Policy. It then proposes additions or clarifications to those roles, as well as how these various contributions to fiscal management of PPPs can be coordinated through a proposed Technical Committee.

Responsibilities for Managing PPP FCs as Defined in the PPP Policy

Under the PPP Policy, the Ministry of Finance and Economic Planning (MoFEP) is spearheading the development of the PPP program through its Public Investment Division (PID). PID is responsible for developing the legal, regulatory, and institutional framework for the program, and for issuing standardized PPP provisions and manuals or guidelines for effective management of PPP projects. Two PID units—the Project and Financial Analysis Unit (PFA) and Project Advisory Unit (PAU)—act as gatekeepers and advisors, respectively, to support and oversee the responsible Ministries, Departments and Agencies (MDAs) that are the contracting authorities (CAs) for PPP projects.

Box 3.1 describes the roles of the MDAs relevant to managing FCs of PPPs, as currently stipulated in the PPP Policy. These include the responsibilities of CAs and of the two central units in PID. They also include roles for two additional divisions within MoFEP, the Debt Management Division and the Budget Division, capturing the need to ensure consistency of FCs to PPPs with broader public financial management.

Box 3.1

Roles of MDAs as Specified Under PPP Policy

Contracting Authorities (CAs): CAs, which may include Ministries, Departments or Agencies (MDAs), Metropolitan, Municipal and District Assemblies (MMDAs), and State-Owned Enterprises (SOEs), are the implementing entities for PPPs—that is, the signatories to PPP contracts from the government side. Under the PPP Policy, these entities are required to develop capability in PPP development, with support from PAU. Where appropriate, CAs, especially sector ministries, are encouraged to set up Project Management Units (PMUs), to assist in the project identification, needs and options analysis, initial definition of the PPP concept, and PPP contract management.

Project and Financial Analysis Unit (PFA): PFA is a unit within the PID of MoFEP responsible for analysis of all public investment projects, including PPPs. As per the PPP Policy, the PFA serves as the secretariat to the PPP Approval Committee and is responsible for coordinating all activities required within and outside of MoFEP as part of the gatekeeping review and approval process. The specific functions of the PFA under the PPP Policy are to

- Screen PPP projects to ensure consistency with the National Infrastructure Plan (NIP) and government policy
- Verify that the use of the PPP option is preferable and beneficial relative to direct public investment
- Ensure financial viability and economic soundness value for money (VfM) of PPP projects
- Examine the robustness of PPP contracts over the long term before they are signed
- Ensure compliance with good PPP procurement processes
- Oversee the management and compliance of PPP agreements/concessions.

PPP Advisory Unit (PAU): The PAU is also a unit within the PID of MoFEP. Based on the PPP Policy, the role of PAU is to promote the flow of bankable, viable, and sustainable PPP projects that further the PPP Policy and program. The PAU has the following responsibilities:

- Provide advice and support to CAs to enhance the identification, preparation of feasibility analysis, structuring, negotiation, and procurement of PPP projects
- Build capacity among public sector stakeholders to enable them to lead the implementation of a PPP project from start to finish in a professional and technically competent manner
- Promote awareness and understanding of Ghana's PPP program, to encourage the use of PPP for appropriate projects
- Act as a center of excellence for PPPs in Ghana
- Provide assistance to MDAs and other CAs that want to promote PPPs in their respective sectors and develop, in collaboration with the PFA, model agreements for that sector
- Assist MDAs and other CAs in understanding approval requirements for PPPs, and develop necessary documents for review.

(box continues on next page)

Box 3.1 **Roles of MDAs as Specified Under PPP Policy** *(continued)*

Debt Management Division (DMD): The PPP Policy outlines that the DMD within MoFEP should help ensure fiscal sustainability for PPP projects, considering both direct and CLs for the government, including guarantees, arising from each PPP project. Specifically, the DMD is responsible for

- Fiscal impact: assessing and managing the long-term fiscal risks and impact of PPP projects (direct or contingent, explicit or implicit) and determining whether they are acceptable, given other national priorities
- Government support: confirming the appropriateness of PPPs for sovereign guarantees (debt or specific-event) or other kinds of government support.

Budget Division (BD): Based on the PPP Policy, the BD of MoFEP will establish processes to incorporate PPP project developments into the annual budgeting exercise, and fund direct as well as contingent (unanticipated) calls on the budget. The BD will therefore ensure that any payments to be made by MDAs under the PPP contract are consistent with the national budget.

PPP Approval Committee (PPP AC): The PPP Policy establishes an Approval Committee, responsible for approving PPP projects at key points in the development process (according to a defined approval process, described further in chapter 4). This is a cross-MDA committee, chaired by the Minister of Finance and Economic Planning.

Source: The National Policy on PPPs (GoG 2011a).

Proposed Roles and Responsibilities for Managing FCs from PPPs

Managing FCs from PPPs involves contributions by several government entities, as described above. This includes the MDAs and other government entities that are the direct CAs for PPPs. It also includes several divisions of MoFEP—both those within the PID that are directly responsible for the PPP Program (the PFA and the PAU), and those that are more broadly responsible for prudent public financial management, such as the DMD, the BD, and others.

To ensure that fiscal management of PPPs is well coordinated, it is important that the respective roles of these entities, and how they will work together throughout the PPP development and implementation process, are clear. To that end, this chapter builds on the roles currently set out in the PPP Policy to define in more detail the responsibilities of each entity (including some entities not mentioned in the Policy). Table 3.1 summarizes these roles, highlighting responsibilities during the PPP development and approval process (as described in chapter 4) and the PPP implementation process (chapter 5). The following paragraphs describe these roles in more detail.

Table 3.1 Summary of FC Proposed Institutional Roles

Entity	Role during PPP preparation/approval	Role during PPP implementation
Contracting Authority (CA)	– Identify and estimate cost of FC as part of project preparation (with support from specialist transaction advisors)	– Regularly obtain FC tracking info from PPP sponsor – Monitor and respond to FC-related project risks – Include FC payments in budget requests submitted to government
Ministry of Finance and Economic Planning: Public Investment Division		
Project Advisory Unit (PAU)	– Support and quality assure the above process – Help develop standard contractual clauses and other guidance material on FC	
Project and Financial Analysis Unit (PFA)	– Coordinate assessment and approval of PPP, including FC – Act as secretariat for FCTC	– Oversee PPP monitoring undertaken by the CA – Feed updated FC estimates into reporting and budgeting
State-Owned Enterprise (SOE) Unit	– Assess and advise on SOE financial health and exposure to PPP commitments as member of FCTC for relevant projects	– Monitor SOE performance including for PPP contracts – Review implications for GoG expenditure and the need for any budget transfers
Other Ministry of Finance and Economic Planning Divisions		
Debt Management Division (DMD)	– Assess and advise on FC liabilities from a **liability management** point of view as member of FCTC	– Monitor impact of PPP FCs (particularly contingent) on liability management – Incorporate updated FC estimates into debt analysis and reports
Budget Division (BD)	– Assess and advise on FC affordability from a **budget priorities/constraints** point of view, as member of FCTC	– Incorporate FC as needed into relevant reports – Allocate and release budget for direct payments and realized CL – Allocate contingency budget for CL obligations
Economic Research and Forecasting Division (ERFD)	– Assess and advise on PPP projects' FC from an **overall liability and macro management** view point, as member of FCTC	– Where relevant, incorporate updated PPP liabilities in macro/ fiscal projections

Source: World Bank data.
Note: CL = contingent liabilities; FC = fiscal commitments; FCTC = Fiscal Commitment Technical Committee; GoG = Government of Ghana; PPP = public-private partnership.

It is proposed that coordination of fiscal management of PPPs is facilitated by a Fiscal Commitment Technical Committee (FCTC). Membership of the FCTC will comprise representatives of all the MoFEP units and divisions with a role to play in managing PPP FCs, as listed below. The FCTC would aggregate feedback on the FCs under a proposed PPP into a single set of recommendations, to be submitted to the relevant PPP approving body for the project (as described further in chapter 4).

Contracting Authorities (CAs): As noted in the PPP Policy, the CA has primary responsibility for developing PPP projects in the sector under its remit, supported by its specialist advisors. It is also responsible for implementing and managing ongoing PPPs. This means that the CA is primarily responsible for ensuring that FCs are identified and evaluated as part of the project development work (typically by ensuring that the requirement to do so is built into the Terms of Reference for consultants, as described further in chapter 4). The CA will also be responsible for obtaining from the concessionaire in a timely manner the performance data needed to track and monitor FCs (such as tariff revenue data in the case of a minimum revenue guarantee (MRG), or overall financial performance measures), and for responding to emerging risks with fiscal implications. Finally, the CA will need to build budget requirements for PPP projects into its annual budget requests.

Project Advisory Unit (PAU): The role of the PAU is to provide technical assistance to the CAs in developing and recommending PPP projects for approval. This will include ensuring that FCs are identified and addressed appropriately in prefeasibility and feasibility studies. Over time, the PAU will also help develop standard tools and guidelines—such as standard risk allocation matrices and PPP agreements—that will influence decision-making regarding FCs under PPPs.

Project Financial Analysis Unit (PFA): The PFA is the PPP "gatekeeper," in that it is responsible for coordinating the PPP approval process. This includes checking that all necessary analysis of a PPP project has been done to an adequate standard, to feed into project approval. This will extend to ensuring that the fiscal implications of a project have been carefully evaluated, and coordinating inputs from the FCTC at appropriate stages of the PPP development process. During PPP implementation, the PFA is the primary source of central guidance, support, and oversight to CAs on contract monitoring, management, and evaluation, with a focus on defending the public interest. This will include ensuring that the necessary data on all PPP projects with fiscal implications are collected from CAs and shared with the relevant entities outlined in this report.

Debt Management Division (DMD): Building on the DMD's mandate to manage the government's debt sustainably, the DMD will ensure that PPP FCs are acceptable from a liability management point of view, and build those commitments into its overall monitoring and reporting on the government's liabilities. Box 3.2 describes why DMD has a key role in managing PPP FCs. During PPP project development, the DMD, as part of the FCTC, will provide recommendations on how the proposed FCs would impact the Government of Ghana's (GoG's) overall liability portfolio (for example, how they would impact on Debt Sustainability Analysis, or DSA) and whether this impact is acceptable. On an ongoing basis, the DMD will also monitor the government's overall portfolio of PPP-related liabilities, and build these estimates into their assessment and reporting on the government's overall indebtedness. The DMD's Domestic Debt Unit will also have a specific contribution on assessing and monitoring PPPs undertaken by SOEs, as described further below.

Box 3.2

Role of Debt Offices in Managing Liabilities from PPPs

The DMD's overall mandate is to source, administer, and manage the public and quasi-public debts and to develop strategies for effective public debt management. On the face of it, this would appear to make minimal DMD's involvement in PPPs, which often entail private rather than public borrowing. However, there are two reasons why the DMD has an important role to play in managing PPP FCs. In practice, the DMD has already expressed its commitment to monitoring and reporting on a wider range of GoG financial commitments.[a]

First, Debt Management Offices (DMO) or Departments often take a role in managing the government's *contingent liabilities*. Common rationales for debt offices undertaking the task of assessing the risks associated with CL such as guarantees are as follows: (1) the similarities between the expertise needed to manage contingent debt with the expertise available in DMOs with the issuance of debts and their financial management (for example, risk quantification, coordination of the conventional and guaranteed debt issuance in the market by way of managing funding risk; obtaining contingency loans); and (2) the need to manage the risks associated with the CLs by adjustments in conventional debt because of the rigidity of the guarantee portfolio, given their linkages to specific projects or borrowers and hence overall illiquidity. In Colombia, Morocco, New Zealand, Slovenia, and Sweden, this function is integratated in the DMO.

Second, long-term *direct liabilities* to PPP contracts, such as availability payments or annuities, create annual obligations that are very similar to public debt. For that reason, some measure of these liabilities is often captured in recording and reporting of public debt, as described further in chapter 5. This means the implications for public debt and liability management may be key to the decision-making process of a proposed PPP.

Source: Cebotari 2008.
a. As noted in the MTDS for 2011–13. "It is intended to extend the scope (of the public debt portfolio) of coverage to guaranteed or non-guaranteed and all other financial transactions which has direct or indirect financial obligation on government" (GoG 2011–13).

Budget Division (BD): The BD will assess and provide inputs to FCTC recommendations on the consistency of a proposed PPP's fiscal implications with budget priorities and constraints. As described further in chapter 4, this will include considering the impact of a new PPP on the annual budget and Medium Term Expenditure Framework (MTEF), as well as assessing the possible longer-term implications, such as increased budget rigidity, particularly in the case of a PPP that creates annual payment obligations over a long period. During PPP implementation, the BD will have a key role in ensuring that PPP FCs are adequately budgeted for, as described in chapter 5. To this end, the BD will liaise with the PID and DMD to ensure that annual direct commitments or realized CLs under PPPs are reflected adequately in the relevant CA's budget, and that an adequate contingency is budgeted for ongoing PPP CLs.

Box 3.3

Functions of the ERF Division

The role of the ERF Division is to provide high-level capacity for research, forecasting, and analysis of macro strategies for MoFEP. The Division's objectives are to (1) conduct macro-economic research on relevant issues affecting the economy; (2) systematically review and analyze existing policies and formulate new ones to improve management of the economy; (3) regularly report on the state of the economy; (4) provide research, technical, and analytical support with respect to local government fiscal matters and intergovernmental finance relations; and (5) enhance policy decision making through forecasting and the maintenance of a macroeconomics database. In doing so, the ERF Division liaises with several other MDAs through the Economic Policy Coordinating Committee (EPCC).

Finally, the BD will disclose the relevant information on FCs from PPPs in the Budget Statement presented annually to Parliament.

SOE Unit in PID and Domestic Debt Unit in DMD: As previously noted, a number of SOEs are likely to undertake PPPs, which in many cases create long-term obligations to purchase services from the private sector—such as under power and water purchase agreements. In these cases, the fiscal implications for the GoG depend on broader SOE governance, and financial and operational performance—whether or not the GoG provides an explicit guarantee on the payment obligations of the SOE under the PPP. The responsibilities in GoG for SOE oversight are still evolving. Within MoFEP, the PID includes a new SOE Unit with a mandate for SOE oversight that is at an early stage (currently comprising one staff member). Additionally, the DMD's Domestic Debt Unit is responsible for assessing SOEs that obtain government guarantees on their commercial loans. A State Enterprise Commission (SEC) is a corporate entity that also has a remit covering SOE performance. As these responsibilities crystallize, a coordinated approach to the assessment and oversight of SOEs undertaking PPPs is needed; for now, the SOE Unit and DMD should feed into the FCTC recommendations for PPPs undertaken by SOEs as necessary.

Economic Research and Forecasting (ERF) Division: The National Policy on PPPs did not explicitly outline the role of the ERF Division of MoFEP. However, the ERF Division is included here for two reasons: to ensure that economic forecasts relevant to the assessment of PPP commitments feed into the process in a coordinated way; and conversely, to ensure that data on PPPs feed into ERF reporting and analysis functions (described in box 3.3) as appropriate.

CHAPTER 4

Managing FCs—PPP Development Stage

The most important aspect of managing fiscal commitments (FCs) under public-private partnership (PPP) projects is deciding which commitments to accept in the first place. Several key aspects of this decision—such as structuring the PPP and allocating risks and responsibilities—are outside the scope of this report, as described in chapter 2. This chapter focuses on how the Government of Ghana (GoG) can ensure that the potential fiscal cost of a proposed PPP is well understood and carefully assessed as a PPP project is being developed, and that this assessment feeds into the PPP approval process.

The PPP Policy sets out a clear process for approving PPP projects. Figure 4.1 summarizes the PPP approval process, which entails four approval stages. The first is approval by the sector minister of a PPP "pre-feasibility study" (PFS) (Approval I in the policy). This is followed by approvals for: the Feasibility Study (FS) (Approval II); bidding documents and evaluation reports (Approvals III-A and III-B); and the final contract and PPP management plan (Approval IV). As shown in figure 4.1, the latter approvals are granted by the relevant contracting authority (CA)—depending on the project size and other characteristics,[1] this authority could be the Public Investment Division (PID), the PPP Approval Committee,[2] Cabinet, or Parliament.

The proposed PPP Law is expected to further embed the PPP approval process set out in figure 4.1.[3] In particular, the PPP Law will help clear up some remaining ambiguities about how current public financial management legislation affects PPP approval requirements. As described in box 4.1, the questions of whether and when "guarantees" under PPP arrangements will require parliamentary approval are particularly relevant to managing FCs under PPPs.

Sound FC management requires that assessment of the FCs under a proposed PPP feeds into PPP approvals at each stage. Accordingly, figure 4.2 augments the approval process of figure 4.1, highlighting the FC management process at each stage of PPP development and approval:

- The PFS, prepared by the CA with support from Project Advisory Unit (PAU) for approval by the sector minister, should include an initial estimate of the

Figure 4.1 The PPP Approval Process in Accordance with the PPP Policy

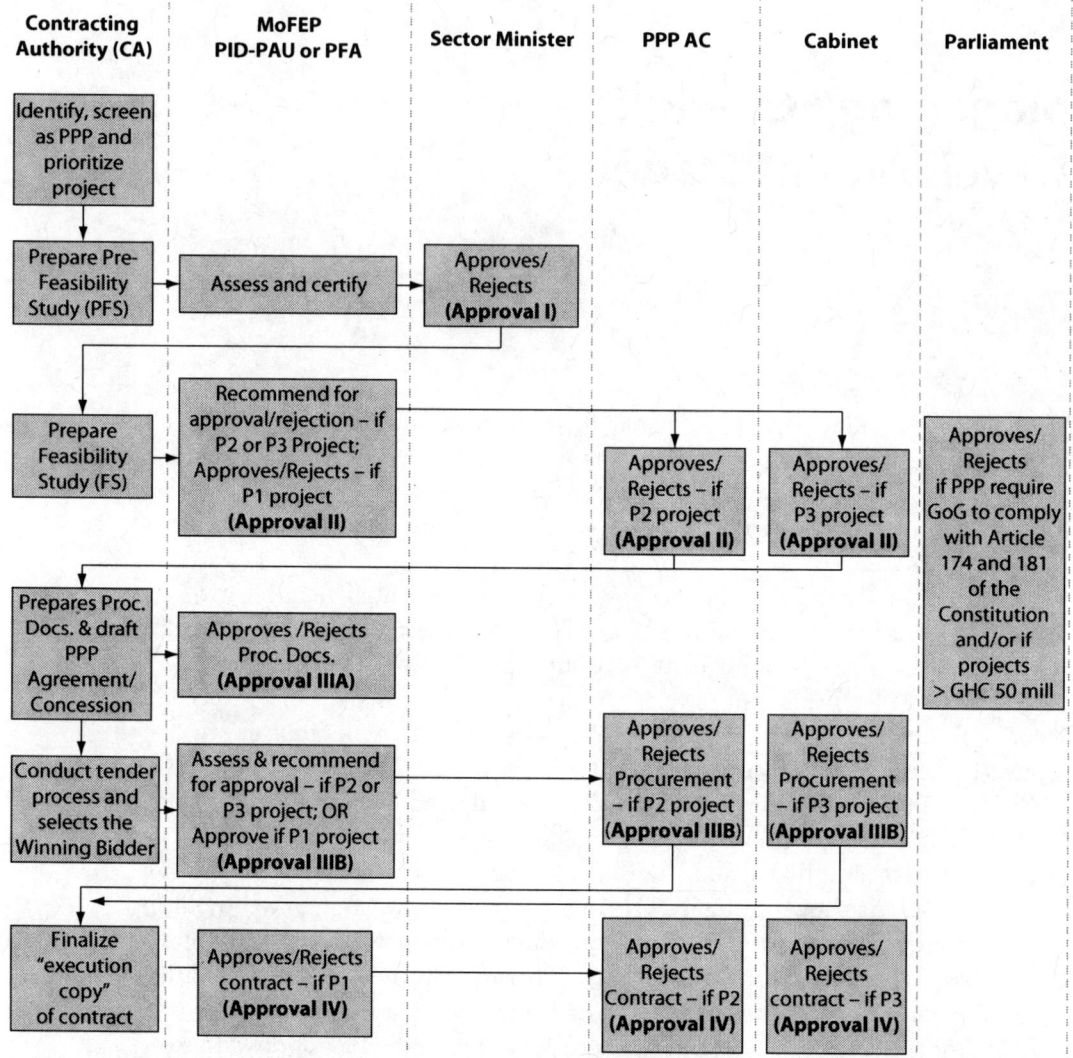

Note: Project approval breakdown as per the PPP Policy: P1: if Project Cost < GHC 2 million; P2: if Project Cost > GHC 2 million & < GHC 50 million; & P3: if Project Cost > GHC 50 million; AC = Approval Committee; GHC = Ghanaian Cedi; GoG = Government of Ghana; PAU = Project Advisory Unit; PFA = Project and Financial Analysis Unit; PID = Public Investment Division; PPP = public-private partnership.

overall required government support—that is, any subsidy that the GoG may need to pay—and should identify major project risks.

- This assessment develops through the FS, which should include developing the PPP structure in sufficient detail to also estimate the cost of the resultant FCs (as described further in chapter 4). At this stage, an Fiscal Commitment Technical Committee (FCTC) review should be required, and a report on the FCTC analysis and recommendations provided to the relevant approving body.

Box 4.1

Public Financial Management Legislation Relevant to PPP FC Management

Current public financial management legislation that may affect the PPP approval process includes the 1992 Constitution, the Loans Act (1970), and the Financial Administration Act (2003). The proposed PPP Law is intended in part to clarify how the requirements of these pieces of legislation—particularly requirements for parliamentary approvals—apply to PPPs. For example, this includes defining whether an "international business or economic transaction to which the government is a party," which under Article 181 of the Constitution as well as the Loans Act of 1970 (Act 335) requires parliamentary approval, would include PPPs.

Of particular relevant to managing FCs under PPPs is the provision in the Loans Act (Act 335) that requires parliamentary approval of all "Government Guarantees." Clarification is needed as to whether this applies only to GoG guarantees on loans, or whether it also applies to other types of "guarantees" common under PPP arrangements, such as MRGs or GoG guarantees of payment obligations of State-Owned Enterprises (SOEs) under PPP projects.

- The actual level of FC under a PPP project will often not be known until the tender process has been carried out and the winning bidder has been selected—particularly where a FC such as a level of subsidy is among the bid criteria. FCTC review will again feed into the relevant approval at this stage.
- Finally, it is possible that FCs may change after selection of the winning bidder and before achieving the "finalized execution copy of the contract" (although the bid process should aim to minimize negotiation at this stage). A final FCTC review of the FCs may be needed at this stage if the FCs have changed significantly.

At each stage, the FCTC review should include inputs from each of the entities involved in managing FCs under PPPs, as described under chapter 3. The following sections describe in more detail what is involved in identifying and evaluating FCs to PPPs, and in considering the affordability of those commitments in light of budget and liability management constraints.

Identifying and Evaluating FCs to PPPs

The first step in assessing the fiscal implications of a proposed PPP is to identify and evaluate the cost of the FCs implied by the project structure. The CA, in collaboration with the PAU, should be able to determine at the PFS whether or

Figure 4.2 Integrating FC Management in the PPP Development and Approval Stage

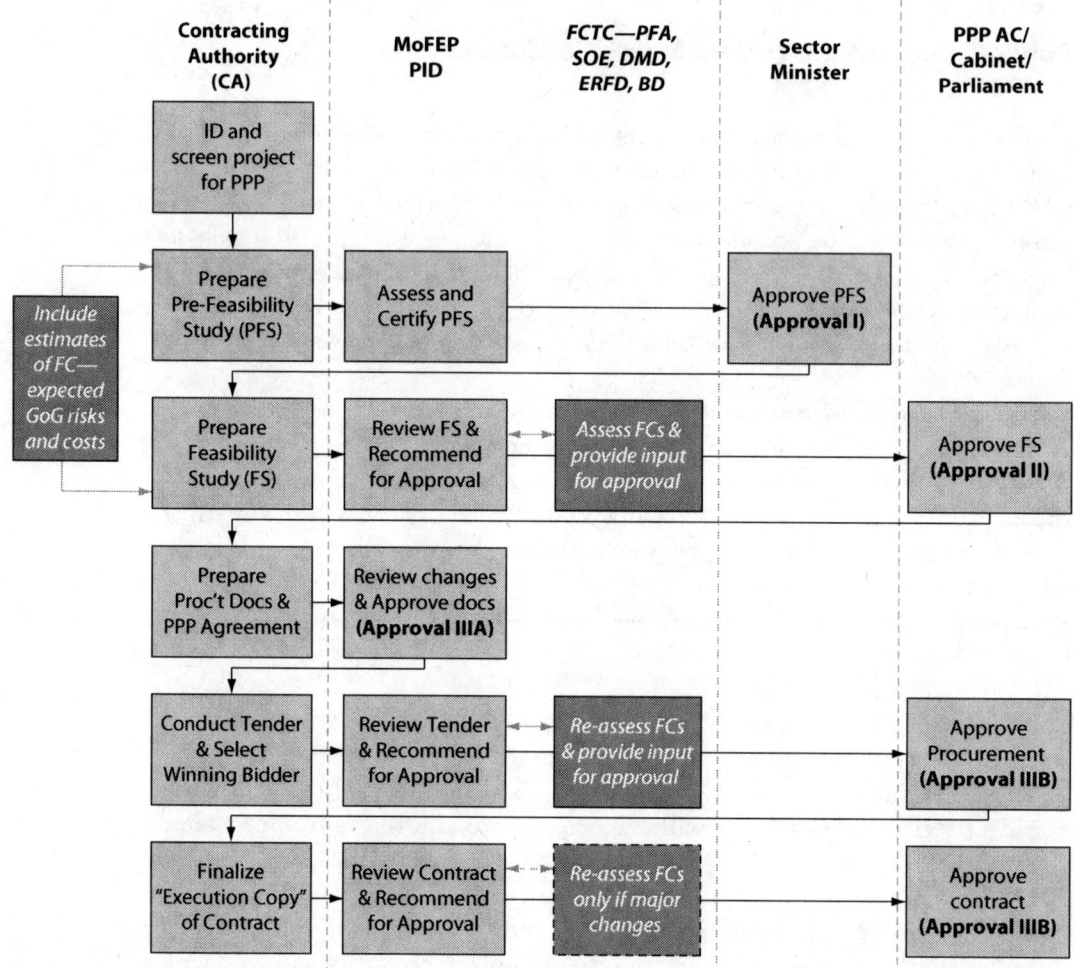

Note: BD = Budget Division; DMD = Debt Management Division; ERFD = Economic Research and Forecasting Division; FC = Fiscal Commitment; FCTC = Fiscal Commitment Technical Committee; GoG = Government of Ghana; MoFEP = Ministry of Finance and Economic Planning; PFA = Project and Financial Analysis Unit; PID = Public Investment Division; PPP = Public-Private Partnership; SOE = State-Owned Enterprise.

not there is a need for government support. However, the details of the proposed PPP structure—and in turn the FCs that the GoG will accept under the PPP—will not be known until the FS stage. The CA and PAU should ensure that the relevant information and analysis are specified in the terms of reference (TOR) for the advisors that will undertake the FS.

The process of "identifying" FCs stems from the process of structuring the PPP. This includes the following: allocating risks (and hence, identifying which risks are borne by the government, creating a FC); defining payment mechanisms, including payments for services required by government; and defining responsibilities, which may include government responsibilities such as the provision of linking infrastructure that will have a fiscal cost. This information should be drawn together in the FS to present a complete picture of the government's liabilities under the proposed PPP structure, as well as their likely costs as described further below.

Evaluating the cost of FCs is typically a corollary of building the financial model of the project. A financial model will typically involve developing different scenarios for the financial performance of the project under different sets of assumptions. The same information can be used to calculate the cost to government of the PPP—for example, payments from the government to the concessionaire would not only be part of the "income" for the project financial model but also constitute part of the fiscal cost of the project.

There are several possible "measures" for expressing the cost of FCs under PPP projects. In the case of direct FCs, this typically includes both the estimated annual value and the present value of the stream of payment commitments over the project lifetime. Evaluating the cost of contingent liabilities (CLs) is more complex, since the timing and value of payments are uncertain. Box 4.2 sets out some broad options for this evaluation.

Box 4.2

Assessing the Cost of Contingent Liabilities

Evaluating the cost of CLs is challenging given that the need for, timing, and value of payments are uncertain. In general, there are two possible approaches:[a]

- **Scenario analysis** involves making assumptions regarding the outcome of any events or variables that affect the value of the CL and calculating the cost given those assumptions. This could include working out the cost to government in a "worst case" scenario. For instance, for a MRG for a road PPP, this assessment would include calculating the cost at different levels of traffic outturn. It could also include calculating the cost to the government of contract terminations for different reasons.
- **Probabilistic analysis** is an alternative approach that uses a formula to define how the variables that affect the value of the CL will behave. Probabilistic analysis treats all input parameters as variables that change according to an assigned probability distribution function. The probability distribution predicts the likely behavior of an input parameter over a range of potential input parameter values. This approach enables estimation of a distribution of possible costs and calculation of measures such as the median (most likely) cost, the mean (average) cost, and different percentiles (for example, the 90th percentile, or the value within which the cost is likely to lie 90 percent of the time). This approach requires a lot of information on the underlying risk variables.[b]

A scenario analysis approach is likely to be the most relevant for the GoG, as it is a simpler way of analyzing risk. It gives a sense of the range of possible outcomes, but not their

(box continues on next page)

Box 4.2 Assessing the Cost of Contingent Liabilities *(continued)*

likelihoods, which can be assessed qualitatively. In practice, most governments that assess the possible cost of CLs employ the scenario analysis approach. A probabilistic approach requires more input data and complex statistical analysis. Only a few governments use probabilistic analysis, and can only apply it to some types of CLs (such as Chile's assessment of MRGs on toll road projects).[c]

a. WBI PPP Reference Guide V1.
b. Appendix A in Irwin (2003) provides an example of how to value revenue guarantees and variable subsidies.
c. See Irwin and Mokdad (2009) for a description of this approach.

The best approach to evaluating FCs to PPPs strikes a balance between simplicity of analysis and an appropriate consideration of risks. Table 4.1 suggests the type of measures that could be built into the TORs for PPP feasibility studies for different types of PPP FCs.

Table 4.1 Suggested FC Analysis in PPP Feasibility Studies

Type of FC	Suggested analysis
All PPP projects	*Total value of PPP project debt*
Direct fiscal support (for example, availability payments)	• **Annual cost** over the project life (both up-front and ongoing commitments) • **Present value** of the payment stream for long-term commitments Both values should be calculated under "base case" assumptions, and under "downside" scenarios for key assumptions.
Guarantees on particular risk variables (for example, demand or exchange rate guarantees)	At a minimum, a scenario analysis approach should include the following: • **Estimated annual cost** under different scenarios for each guaranteed risk variable (base case, and downside scenarios) • **"Trigger points"** for relevant risk variables—that is, the change from the base case at which CLs become payable (for example, % drop in demand from base case at which a demand guarantee is payable), and qualitative analysis of the likelihood of reaching these values Over time, and for variables where the GoG is building up significant exposure, could move toward probabilistic approach (to determine "expected" value and range).
Payment guarantees (that is, guarantee on payment by SOE)	Value of underlying payment requirements ("face value" of guarantee), in terms of the following: • **Annual cost** over the project life • **Present value** of the payment stream Analysis of transfers likely to be required to meet payments under different scenarios for key variables (for example, sector tariffs) and a qualitative estimate of likelihood for each scenario.
Termination payment commitments (payments in case of contract termination by either party)	• **Maximum value** of the termination payment, under base case assumptions (Value will vary over the project lifetime; maximum typically at project commissioning, when debt has been drawn down and repayments have not started) • For any termination payments triggered by concessionaire default, **"trigger points"** for relevant key assumptions at which default might occur (for example, % drop in demand that would mean insufficient cash for debt service), and a qualitative analysis of the risk of default.

Source: World Bank and Castalia 2011.

Assessing Affordability of PPP FCs as an Input to Approval

Having estimated the cost of PPP FCs, the government needs to decide whether those commitments are affordable and fiscally responsible. Even if a PPP project is found to be economically viable and has been structured to provide value for money (VfM), the GoG needs to check that it can afford the associated FCs in light of its fiscal constraints. Generally, this can be achieved by the following: (1) comparing annual cost estimates against the projected budget of the CA; (2) considering the impact on debt sustainability; and/or (3) introducing specific limits on different types of PPP commitments.[4]

Assessing the affordability of proposed PPP FCs in light of *budget* constraints and priorities is the responsibility of the Budget Division (BD). At a minimum, this assessment should compare the estimated annual cost of the FCs (whether direct or contingent) with the annual budget of the relevant sector. This may involve projecting forward sector spending over the lifetime of the PPP contract—in the absence of a long-term expenditure plan, the simplest approach is to assume growth in sector spending beyond the end of the Medium Term Expenditure Framework (MTEF) equal to overall economic growth. Without a hard-and-fast rule as to what can be considered "affordable," as described in the following paragraph, this analysis should focus on avoiding excessive budget rigidity by overcommitting too high a proportion of resources in any given sector. The budget implication of the "worst-case" contingent liability scenarios should also be considered—for example, by estimating the maximum possible payment in case of termination as a percentage of the GoG's overall budget and discretionary budget to consider the degree of fiscal flexibility that would be required should this liability be realized.

Assessing the affordability of FCs under a PPP project in terms of the government's overall *liability* management is primarily the responsibility of the Debt Management Division (DMD). At a minimum, the DMD should consider whether the PPP debt will need to be recognized as a public liability and included in debt measures (as described in chapter 5), and determining the impact on overall debt sustainability. The DMD should also consider the size of the government's commitments under the PPP contract—both regular payments and CLs—and how these compare and contribute to the government's existing liabilities portfolio. In this regard, the Economic Research and Forecasting Division (ERFD) should also consider whether and how the GoG's liabilities under the PPP may affect its fiscal projections and analysis.

Some governments introduce specific limits on FCs to PPPs, either as part of the spending commitments of the specific department or in aggregate for the PPP program (see box 4.3 for some examples). Generally, the rationale for such limits is to avoid tying up too much of the budget (whether at the sector or aggregate level) in long-term payment commitments. Given that rationale, such a limit is not typically necessary in the very early stages of a PPP program. This position could be reconsidered in Ghana as initial PPP projects are executed

---

Box 4.3

Country Examples of Limits on FCs to PPPs

Some countries have introduced explicit limits on PPP FCs. The United Kingdom, for example, has specified individual Departmental Spending Limits for each department, ranging from 6 to 7 percent of total annual spending. Brazil's current PPP law prohibits undertaking new PPPs if the projected stream of payments under the overall PPP program exceeds 1 percent of government revenue in any future year. In Greece, the current payments of approved PPP projects account for 6–7 percent of its Public Investments Program, are expected to reach 10–12 percent in five years, and are ultimately capped at a limit of 15 percent.

In India, an Inter-Ministerial Task Force was constituted to recommend budgetary ceilings for annuity commitments under PPP projects. The Task Force's September 2010 report proposed that the sum of total annuity commitments for a particular grant or scheme of any Ministries, Departments and Agencies (MDA) for the next five years should not exceed 25 percent of the Department's current Five Year Plan outlay of such grant or scheme. However, no cap is set for guarantees issued to PPPs.[a]

a. India Planning Commission Task Force Report (2010).

---

and GoG has a better idea of the potential and scope of its PPP program, and of the type of support it is likely to provide to its PPPs, such as annuities, guarantees, and/or up-front financial support.

Table 4.2 summarizes key "ratios" that can be used to assess the affordability of a proposed PPP from both budget and liability management perspectives. That is, it sets out how the DMD and BD can use the information on the cost of each FC calculated in the FS, to think about the affordability of the PPP. For the BD, this involves comparing annual costs with the funds available (in relevant sector budgets, and at an overall level in considering how CLs will be budgeted for and their possible impact if realized unexpectedly). For the DMD, this involves comparing the overall size of each liability in present value terms with the existing debt stock. To calculate these present values (PVs), the DMD will need to choose an appropriate discount rate. A default option could be the GoG's external borrowing cost for long-term loans.[5] The measures in table 4.2 may also be used for monitoring and reporting on PPP FCs during the implementation stage, as described in chapter 5.

Where a PPP project is being undertaken by an SOE, the fiscal impact assessment needs to take into consideration the broader financial position of the SOE, and so the input of the PID SOE Unit and the Domestic Debt Department of the DMD will be important. In this case, the PPP creates a CL for the GoG, whether explicit or implicit (as described in paragraph 13). The likelihood and cost of the GoG needing to make payments depends on the financial obligations

Table 4.2 Key Ratios on Affordability Assessment and Risk Exposure from PPPs

FC type	Relevant measure	Relevant comparator for considering affordability
Budget implications		
Long-term direct FCs (for example, availability payments)	Annual payment	The relevant measure as a percentage of Sector/ MDA budget *(projected forward from end of MTEF if necessary)*
Guarantees (for example, on particular risk variables such as demand; or for payment guarantees)	Estimated annual payment— "base" and "downside" cases Contingency budget required *(see chapter 5 on budgeting)*	The relevant measure as a percentage of Sector/ MDA budget *(projected forward from end of MTEF if necessary)* The relevant measure as a percentage of "Contingency" line The relevant measure as a percentage of total and discretionary annual budget
Termination payments or other CLs that could require one-off payment	"Worst case" payment Contingency budget required *(see chapter 5 on budgeting)*	The relevant measure as a percentage of "Contingency" line; % of total and discretionary annual budget *(to consider impact of having to make sudden payment)*
Liability management implications		
All PPPs Long-term direct FCs (for example, availability payments)	Value of PPP debt PV of GoG payments	
Guarantees on particular risk variables	PV of annual payments—"base" and "downside" cases	The relevant measure as a percentage of total public debt exposure; and % of GDP *(to consider impact on debt sustainability and liability position of adding the proposed commitment)*
"Payment" guarantees	PV of underlying payment stream ("face value" of guarantee) PV of payments under different scenarios	
Termination payments	Maximum payment required (typically = debt + equity)	

Source: World Bank data.
Note: FC = fiscal commitment; MDA = Ministries, Departments and Agencies; MTEF = Medium Term Expenditure Framework; CLs = contingent liabilities; PPP = public-private partnership; PV = present value; GoG = Government of Ghana; GDP = gross domestic product.

of the SOE under the PPP contract, and also on the overall financial position of the SOE (which affects the likelihood that a transfer from the GoG will be needed to meet those obligations).

For example, for a "take-or-pay" type agreement with an Independent Power Producer (IPP) or a bulk water supplier, this could include considering how the cost of power or water under the agreement compares with the increase in retail tariff revenue that the relevant SOE—Volta River Authority (VRA) or Ghana Water Company Limited (GWCL), respectively—can expect to receive as a result of the increased supply. This might include considering different scenarios for key variables such as exchange rates (since retail tariffs are denominated in Ghanaian Cedi, while purchase agreements are typically denominated in the investors' currency). The MoFEP should also note any commitments under the PPP contract that would require action by other GoG entities—such as providing additional power connections to a new water treatment plant—and clarify how the cost of these actions will be met.

As noted in the introduction to this chapter, the views of each entity regarding the FCs for a proposed PPP should be drawn together into an FCTC recommendation to the relevant PPP project approving body. The aim is to ensure a consistent view on the affordability of the PPP project. The Project and Financial Analysis Unit (PFA), as secretariat of the FCTC, will be responsible for coordinating this joint recommendation in a timely way to feed into the PPP approval at each stage of the process.

Notes

1. The categorization of projects is listed in figure 4.1—denoted as P1, P2, and P3—and is also covered in the PPP Policy in paragraph 52 and in the associated Approval Schedule on page 18.

2. The PPP Approval Committee includes but is not limited to: Minister responsible for Finance (in the Chair), Chairman of the National Development Planning Commission (NDPC), Minister of Justice and Attorney General, Minister of Trade and Industry, Chief Executive of Ghana Investment Promotion Centre, Director of Public Procurement Authority, and Minister of the Contracting Authority of the PPP under consideration (or where there is no sector minister, the head of the contracting authority or his designated representative).

3. For more information on the proposed PPP Law, see the GoG Draft PPP Law Interim Report (March-April 2012). A draft PPP law is expected to be completed and presented to parliament in 2013.

4. WBI PPP Reference Guide V.1

5. Using the government's long-term borrowing cost will yield a PV that is comparable to the size of a loan that would create a similar repayment stream. Adjusting for risk would also be an option—particularly in the case of CLs—but is arguably less appropriate when discounting a stream of costs than a stream of revenues.

CHAPTER 5

Managing FCs—Project Implementation Stage

Many PPP FCs last the duration of the PPP contract. Over that time, the Government of Ghana (GoG) needs to make sure that those commitments are monitored carefully, reported appropriately in government accounts and statistics, and budgeted and paid promptly as needed. The GoG should also keep an eye on its PPP FCs at an overall portfolio level. This chapter sets out each of these elements of managing fiscal commitments (FCs) during project implementation. As noted in chapter 4, there is also feedback between managing PPP FCs at the project development and implementation stages; clarity in how PPP FCs will be accounted and paid for also helps in assessing whether the FCs of a proposed public-private partnership (PPP) are affordable.

Monitoring PPP Fiscal Commitments

To manage, report on, and budget for the FCs arising from PPP projects, the Ministry of Finance and Economic Planning (MoFEP) must maintain an up-to-date record of these commitments, at both the project and portfolio levels. This requires gathering information on project performance from the concessionaire— as well as other inputs that affect the cost of PPP FCs, such as updated projections of key economic variables—and ensuring that this information reaches the relevant entities within MoFEP.

Given its mandate for overseeing the management of PPP contracts, the Project and Financial Analysis Unit (PFA) will be the main conduit of FC monitoring information for MoFEP. Gathering information from the concessionaire is typically the responsibility of the contracting authority (CA), which has the direct contractual relationship with the PPP company/ concessionaire. Information requirements to this end should be clearly specified in the PPP contract—for example, these could include traffic information, and key financial ratios for the PPP Company—along with indicators needed to monitor service performance. To back up this requirement, the PPP Law could include a provision giving the GoG (CA and/or MoFEP) the right to periodically collect monitoring information from the PPP Company, as described in chapter 6.

In its contract monitoring oversight role, the Public Investment Division (PID) should also be alert to emerging risks that could trigger contingent liabilities (CLs). FC monitoring is not simply a passive task, but should include identifying emerging issues that could create fiscal risks, and if necessary, supporting the CA to take action on these issues. This could include coordinating inputs from other Fiscal Commitment Technical Committee (FCTC) entities any time contractual changes are considered. Where the PPP is undertaken by a State-Owned Enterprise (SOE), the PFA will need to work with the SOE Unit to coordinate oversight activities.

Other entities within MoFEP that will need access to FC monitoring information are the Debt Management Division (DMD), Budget Division (BD), and Economic Research and Forecasting Division (ERFD). The DMD should monitor liabilities from PPPs at the portfolio level—maintaining up-to-date estimates of the "ratios" listed in table 4.2—and incorporate this information in reporting and disclosure as described in the following section. The ERF Division may also need FC information to feed into fiscal projections[1] (and, conversely, may need to provide projections for economic variables that feed into assessments of the PPP portfolio by other entities, to ensure consistency). Finally, the BD will require updated information on annual costs to ensure that FCs are adequately budgeted for and built into the Medium Term Expenditure Framework (MTEF), as described in chapter 5. These entities may, in turn, feed back to PID any concerns regarding emerging fiscal risks from PPP contracts.

Reporting on and Disclosure of PPP FCs

Since PPP FCs are often long-term financial liabilities for the government, regular reporting on these commitments is important to provide clarity on the GoG's overall liabilities position. Reporting *within* government ensures that decision makers bear in mind the full range of GoG liabilities when making public financial management decisions. *Public* disclosure of these liabilities fosters transparency and helps build the credibility of the GoG's commitments to its PPP program in the eyes of investors and lenders.

The decisions on when, what, and how to report can be informed by relevant international norms and standards for government financial and statistical reporting. However, there is no single international "best practice." This means the GoG will need to determine its own approach to reporting on and accounting for PPPs, drawing on international approaches as well as its own current approach to reporting and accounting for similar types of liabilities. Doing so in the early stages of the PPP program will be beneficial, since how PPPs are treated in accounts and statistics can have a significant impact on their "affordability."

This section highlights reporting on and disclosure of the fiscal implications of PPP projects for transparency. This is one aspect of ensuring transparency and accountability for the PPP program as a whole. International good practice increasingly involves disclosing information about the structure of PPP projects, whether in the form of the PPP agreements themselves (or part of them) or in a project brief that sets out the key elements of a PPP contract and procurement process. The benefits of releasing this information include greater transparency and accountability, as well as knowledge sharing on PPP structures. Australia is notable for publishing PPP contracts three to six months after financial close (in Partnership Victoria, New South Wales, and Western Australia). Chile also publishes contracts and related documents, including changes made after negotiations.[2]

Recognizing PPP Liabilities in National Accounts and Statistics

The GoG needs to determine whether and when PPP commitments should be recognized—that is, formally recorded in financial statements as a liability. This is particularly important since it defines whether PPP liabilities count towards any GoG debt management limits or targets (such as those determined under the International Monetary Fund [IMF] program). Box 5.1 describes relevant international standards for public accounting and statistics relating to PPP commitments specifically and CLs more broadly. While these standards provide a helpful precedent, the GoG's approach to recognizing PPP liabilities will most likely be guided by IMF requirements. To date, the IMF has not provided any general guidance on how PPP liabilities should be treated in government debt statistics or accounts.

Box 5.1

International Standards for Accounting and Reporting on PPP Commitments

Two types of standards for government accounting and statistics may apply to the FCs of PPP projects: those standards that deal specifically with PPP obligations and those that apply to CLs.

PPP-Specific Standards: International standards for treatment of PPPs in national accounts and statistics focus on whether and when PPP assets and liabilities should be recognized—that is, treated as public assets and debt. In the case of Ghana, the key question is whether PPP project debt should be included as part of reported national debt figures. International standards in this area continue to evolve.

International Public Sector Accounting Standards (IPSAS) Standard 32: Introduced in 2011, Standard 32 applies to governments implementing accrual accounting. Under this standard, PPP assets and liabilities appear on the government's balance sheet provided: (1) the government controls or regulates the services the operator must provide with the PPP asset, to whom, and at what price; and (2) the government controls significant residual interest in the asset at the end of the contract. Under this definition, "government-pays"

(box continues on next page)

Box 5.1 International Standards for Accounting and Reporting on PPP Commitments *(continued)*

PPPs would appear on the government's balance sheet; the treatment of "user-pays" PPPs is less clear, and may depend on the details of the contract. While Ghana has adopted the International Financial Reporting Standards (IFRS) for private sector companies, it has not yet adopted IPSAS for public sector accounting.[a]

Prior to the introduction of IPSAS Standard 32, an oft-cited standard was a Eurostat ruling governing national statistics for EU members, which takes a less conservative approach. Eurostat requires governments to recognize PPP liabilities in government debt statistics only when the government retains both demand and construction risk. Since most PPPs at least transfer construction risk to the private party, under this rule, most PPPs remain off the government's balance sheet.

Standards for Contingent Liabilities: Since many PPP contracts create CLs for the government, international standards for treatment of CLs in national accounts and statistics are also relevant to PPPs. These include International Public Sector Accounting Standards (IPSAS) 19 and the IMF's Government Finance Statistics Manual (IMF 2001). For the most part, these standards do not require liabilities to be recognized in public debt until the contingency is called and cash payments need to be made. The exception is under accrual accounting, where IPSAS 19 requires that the expected cost of contingent obligations be recognized only when (1) it is more likely than not (50 percent) that the event will occur; and (2) the amount of the obligation can be measured sufficiently reliably. International standards and guidance nonetheless encourage disclosure of CLs in national accounts and budget documentation.

Table B5.1.1 Summary of the Main Requirements for Recognition and Disclosures of Contingent Liabilities

		Recongnition	Disclosure
Cash accounting	IPSAS 19	Only when the contingency is called and cash payments need to be made.	Encouraged.
Accrual accounting	IPSAS 19	The expected cost of a contingent obligation should be recognized if: (1) it is more likely then not (50%) that the event will occur; and (2) the amount of the obligation can be measured with sufficient reliability. Liabilities that do not statisfy these criteria should not be recongnized.	Required for the remaining contingent liabilities, unless the likelihood of the payment is remote.
Statistical reporting	GFS 2001	Only when the contingency is called and cash payments need to be made.	Required as a memorandom item to the balance sheet.

Source: Cebotari 2008.

a. http://www.ghana.gov.gh/index.php/news/features/13102-government-to-promote-public-sector-accountability.

Besides direct GoG debt, Ghana's measures of public debt currently include only CLs arising from GoG guarantees on SOE debt. These liabilities are included at face value (that is, the value of the remaining underlying loan) in public debt measures—in particular, as presented in the Medium Term Debt Management Strategy (MTDS 2012–14). This approach is based on the IMF program with GoG and the related Technical Memorandum of Understanding (TMU). The MTDS does not break down debt figures by type; based on a breakdown shared by DMD, GoG guaranteed debt amounted to 1.3 percent of the total foreign debt in 2010, and 2.1 percent in 2009.

Going forward, the GoG may include PPP liabilities for certain types of PPPs in its measures of public debt. Under the GoG's current approach to debt reporting, this would include any PPP where the GoG provides a debt guarantee (whether full or partial)—although such cases should be limited, since other types of fiscal support and risk bearing tend to provide more effective risk allocation. Following international precedent, the treatment of other PPPs will depend on the risk allocation. At a minimum, projects in which the government is bearing both demand and construction risk (following the Eurostat standard) will likely be considered as contributing to government debt.

Reporting on PPP FCs

Even when PPP FCs are not recognized as part of the GoG's debt, they should be reported alongside information and analysis of public debt. As described above, this is important for both internal and external transparency of the government's liability position. Key questions on PPP reporting are what information should be disclosed and where. International standards on CLs provide guidance in this regard. IPSAS and Government Finance Statistics Manual (GFSM) standards encourage disclosing information on CLs in all cases. The IMF Manual on Fiscal Transparency states that budget documentation should include a statement indicating the purpose of each CL, its duration, and the intended beneficiaries, and that major contingencies should be quantified where possible.[3] In practice, the type of CLs disclosed varies across countries—relatively few countries disclose PPP-specific CLs such as revenue or exchange rate guarantees (ERGs).

CLs are disclosed in an increasing number of countries, either in budget documents or other fiscal reports sent to parliament, such as in New Zealand, Australia, a few other Organisation for Economic Co-operation and Development (OECD) countries, and several emerging markets (Brazil, Chile, Colombia, Indonesia, Peru, South Africa). Information on explicit loan guarantees is reported by virtually all countries disclosing CLs, but disclosure of guarantees related to PPP-type arrangements, such as minimum revenue guarantees (MRGs) or ERGs, is more limited (but does occur in Chile, Colombia, Indonesia, Peru, and the United Kingdom).

In Ghana, reporting on PPP FC should include adding information on PPP liabilities alongside public debt reporting in MTDS reports, budget statements, and notes to the national accounts. As the PPP program develops, the government could consider publishing a specific report on PPP commitments (such as the case in Chile, which started by publishing a report on CL from MRG to PPPs—later broadened into a wider CL report that extends beyond PPPs).[4]

The information reported will likely include a mixture of qualitative and quantitative information on the different types of GoG commitments to PPPs. Appendix B provides some sample reporting formats for presenting both direct (long-term) and contingent liabilities under PPP projects. These formats suggest providing a description of liabilities under each PPP project and a simple estimate of the value of the liability. In the case of long-term payment commitments, such as availability payments, the information reported could include the annual cost and the present value (PV) of the payment stream over the contract lifetime. For CLs, the reported information should include any realized costs, as well as the "maximum" or "worst-case" value where this can be calculated.

Over time, depending on the types of commitments the GoG accepts under its PPPs, additional quantitative measures could be reported. For example, for CLs such as MRGs, this could include reporting on the expected cost of guarantees on an annual basis or over the contract lifetime. The Chilean government, for example, discloses information not required by the financial reporting standards it currently follows. In a report on public finances that accompanies the budget, the Chilean government discloses information on the costs of the revenue and exchange-rate guarantees it has granted to toll roads. It presents estimates of the amounts it expects to pay or receive over the next 20 years under the revenue and exchange-rate guarantees, both project by project, and for the overall portfolio.[5]

The GoG should also define how it will treat SOE obligations under PPP contracts in its reporting and accounts. As described in paragraph 14, many PPPs in Ghana may be undertaken by SOEs. In these cases, FCs by the SOE under the PPP contract (such as take-or-pay agreements) can also create fiscal liabilities. Where SOE payments have been *guaranteed* by the GoG, this creates an explicit CL for the GoG that should be reported alongside other CLs under the PPP program.

Where no explicit guarantee has been provided, the GoG may nonetheless have an implicit obligation to support the SOE in case of financial distress, to protect the provision of basic services. This is a more general liability that encompasses all financial obligations of the SOE, not just those under the PPP contract. Specifically reporting on these commitments could risk creating moral hazard: SOEs and the concessionaries could perceive this as explicit government backup, affecting, for example, the private party's due diligence on the capacity of the SOE to meet its PPP commitments. In this case, the clearest approach may be to ensure that SOEs report on their PPP commitments and to reference those reports where the PPP program as a whole is being reported on, while strengthening GoG oversight and visibility of SOE financial performance in general.

Budgeting for PPP FCs

Budgeting appropriately for PPP FCs is important for the reputation of a PPP program. Providing a clear budgeting mechanism to ensure timely payment of both direct and contingent commitments to PPPs improves the credibility of the government's commitments in the eyes of its private partners. If this is not the case and the private party perceives a risk that payments will not be made when due, the cost of this risk will be priced into the PPP contract accordingly— undermining the advantages of a well-designed risk allocation. Ensuring mechanisms are in place for paying for contingent obligations that may be realized unexpectedly also helps reduce the need to make in-year adjustments that negatively affect other budget priorities.

Budgeting for direct, ongoing commitments, such as availability payments or annuities, is relatively straightforward since the timing and value of payments are known. The most common and simplest approach is to build the payment requirement into the annual budget allocation of the relevant Ministries, Departments and Agencies (MDA). As described in chapter 3, the BD is responsible for checking that any PPP CA has built these PPP commitments into its annual budget request, working with the PID and DMD as necessary. Actual payments to PPP companies may be made through a centrally con- trolled account to avoid the risk of delay.

Budgeting for CLs is more challenging, as the need for, timing, and amount of payments are often not known until the liability is realized. If payments are needed unexpectedly and savings cannot be found within the existing appro- priations, the government may need to go to Parliament to request a supple- mentary appropriation—often a slow and contentious process. Other countries have found various ways to reduce this risk—such as creating additional budget flexibility by including a contingency reserve in the budget that can be used to meet calls on CLs, or "insuring" against the need for such payments by creating a fund upfront from which CLs will be paid.[6]

The simplest approach—preferred by the MoFEP BD during discussions in Ghana—is to introduce a "contingency" budget line from which unexpected payments for PPP CLs will be made. This is similar to the approach currently used to deal with CLs from guarantees on SOE lending (for which a contin- gency is built into the annual debt service figure provided to BD by DMD). The annual budget also already includes a government-wide contingency line to cover unexpected spending needs, albeit with a small annual allocation— Ghanaian Cedi (GHC) 282 million in the 2012 budget, or around 2 percent of total spending. It is not clear what this contingency represents. The size of the PPP contingency should be determined by the CLs in the PPP portfolio (taking into account their cost and likelihood of occurrence). The BD will need to work with the PID and DMD to calculate the appropriate allocation in any given year (and to estimate allocations that will be needed over the MTEF period). Over time, MoFEP may develop rules for the level of budget allocation for PPP-related and other types of contingency, reflecting the GoG's level of fiscal risk aversion. If the payments needed in a given year exceed the contingency, budget reprioritizations and supplementary applications may still be needed.

CLs that have already been realized can be treated the same way as direct annual commitments. For example, this could include a revenue guarantee where revenue is expected to be below the guaranteed level (perhaps because this was the case in the previous year). In this case, the amount to be budgeted should correspond to the estimated cost of the guarantee for the relevant fiscal year—again, the BD may need to liaise with the PID and DMD to check that the estimated cost is accurate.

Some countries establish specific funds from which realized CLs will be paid.[7] Such funds can be specific to PPP liabilities (such as in Brazil or Indonesia) or cover a broader set of government CLs. The fund can be actual or notional. *Actual* Reserve Funds (like those in Chile and Colombia) invest resources in financial assets (usually government bonds or Investment Grade/AAA securities), while *Notional* Reserve Funds are government finance accounts to which resources are paid and tracked, but which are pooled into the Treasury's single account and are therefore not invested separately (for example, as in the United States, and the Swedish Guarantee Fund). In either case, the credibility of the fund rests on it being capitalized upfront—creating a high opportunity cost. This approach is unlikely to be justified in Ghana, given the small size of its PPP program.[8]

Notes

1. The roles of the ERF Division include economic research, forecasting, and analysis, as described in chapter 3 (box 3.3). This includes gathering data to forecast the fiscal position of government. In doing so, the ERF Division may apply its own approach to valuing CLs, including from PPPs, which may differ from that used for debt analysis or budgeting (as described in table 4.2). For example, for fiscal forecasting purposes, the value of government guarantees on SOE debt is computed at 25 percent of their face value (as opposed to 100 percent of face value that is reported in debt stock). The choice of 25 percent is not based on any particular assessment of the different SOEs; however, the DMD considers this a conservative estimate given that none of these guarantees have been called.

2. Irwin and Mokdad (2009).

3. Hemming and Staff Team (2006).

4. Government of Chile (2011), Informe de Pasivos Contingentes 2011 (Contingent Liabilities Report, in Spanish), available at http://www.dipres.gob.cl/572/articles-76644_IPC_2011.pdf.

5. Cebotari (2008) and Irwin (2007).

6. Cebotari (2008) also describes other mechanisms used to create additional budget flexibility, such as provisions that allow government *spending in excess of the budget*, within clear restrictions. In OECD countries, such provisions are included in the budget system laws of most countries and in a few instances even in the constitution

(Austria, Finland, the Federal Republic of Germany, and Japan). Another alternative can be to avoid the need for sudden payments through contractual provisions that allow for a time lag between calls on guarantees and government payments (as done, for instance, under concession contracts in Chile). However, these mechanisms are less likely to be feasible in Ghana in the near future.

7. Cebotari (2008).

8. A "hybrid" option could include establishing project-specific escrow accounts. This approach is sometimes demanded by investors to support government guarantees on revenue or debt payments. Each year, the government would maintain in the escrow account the maximum amount needed to cover the guaranteed payment for that fiscal year. This would require a transfer at the start of the project—if the amount is unused, it may be retained in the account against the following year's payments.

CHAPTER 6

Conclusions and Next Steps: Implementing the FC Framework

This report has set out the key elements of a sound framework for managing the fiscal commitments (FCs) from public-private partnership (PPP) projects in Ghana. The overall aim of this framework is to ensure that FCs under PPPs are well understood and managed in a transparent and fiscally responsible way. The framework includes clear institutional responsibilities, principles, and processes to ensure that FCs are carefully considered during project development, managed responsibly, reported on, and budgeted throughout the project lifetime. As noted in the introduction, most elements of this FC framework can be implemented in the short to medium term, as the PPP framework as a whole continues to develop and "first mover" projects under the PPP program are developed and implemented.

Implementing this framework will mean action on several fronts in the short to medium term. These include (1) agreeing on institutional responsibilities and establishing the Fiscal Commitment Technical Committee (FCTC); (2) building the core elements of the FC framework into the proposed PPP Law; (3) building the capacity of the relevant entities as part of the overall PPP capacity-building framework; and (4) beginning to implement the framework in practice for current and forthcoming PPP projects. This chapter briefly describes each of these next steps. Appendix A presents a concise "action plan" that summarizes the main actions and decisions needed in the short term across these fronts and identifies the entities responsible.

Broad agreement on institutional responsibilities within Ministry of Finance and Economic Planning (MoFEP) for managing PPP FCs, as set out in this report, was reached through discussions in Ghana in September 2012. As a next step, MoFEP can establish the proposed FCTC, with the mandate to manage FCs under the PPP program and identify the staff members who will take the lead on implementing the FC actions. At the same time, MoFEP should review and clarify institutional roles for oversight of State-Owned Enterprises (SOEs), and how these will relate to PPPs—particularly since several PPPs currently in development will be undertaken by SOEs.

Several key elements of the FC management framework can be emphasized and clarified by including relevant provisions in the proposed "PPP Law." This law will further develop and entrench many elements of the PPP framework already set out in the PPP Policy and clarify how management of the PPP program relates to other public financial management legislation. Key FC elements that should be built into the PPP Law include the following:

Defining what types of guarantee require parliamentary approval. As described in chapter 4 (box 4.1), the Loans Act (1993) requires parliamentary approval for "government guarantees," but does not distinguish between credit guarantees and other types of guarantees that might be issued under a PPP (such as "take-or-pay" payment guarantees, or a minimum revenue guarantee [MRG]).

Granting MoFEP the right to periodically request and obtain performance information from the contracting authority (CA) and/or the project concessionaire, to ensure that the data for managing FCs are available in a timely manner. The particular data to be provided by a concessionaire on a project can be further elaborated in each PPP contract.

Introducing the obligation for MoFEP to monitor and disclose FCs from PPPs. This is not explicitly required under current legislation, and specifying in law such disclosure requirements for public financial information is common both in Ghana and internationally.[1] This should be in addition to general transparency stipulations, such as minimum disclosure requirements for PPP contractual information.

There is a clear need to build the capacity of staff within the various divisions of MoFEP to undertake the roles assigned in this report. External support from consultants will be crucial in the early stages, as the skills of existing staff are simultaneously augmented. As the PPP program develops, additional staff time may be required to manage the associated work load. Box 6.1 describes likely components of capacity building for managing FCs; these can be integrated into the Government of Ghana's (GoG's) overall capacity-building plan for PPPs.[2]

At the same time, MoFEP can begin introducing elements of the FC framework in practice for current and forthcoming PPP projects. As a first step, this could include taking stock, and gathering and reporting information on FCs from the few existing PPPs (the reporting templates in appendix B could be a useful guide for this exercise). As new PPP projects are developed, FC assessment requirements can be built into the TOR for consultants as described in box 6.1, and questions of how FCs will be monitored, budgeted, and accounted for can be addressed in practice for those projects. Appendix A includes a list of "first-mover" projects for which these measures could be implemented in practice.

In the medium term and as the PPP program develops, the GoG can revisit some aspects of its approach to managing PPP FCs. With the increase in PPP projects, the government will have a better sense of overall scale and the type of viability support and risk mitigation instruments it will be providing. With

---

Box 6.1

Building FC Management Capacity

Building capacity in FC management will be a gradual process, involving both on-the-job training and other capacity-building activities. These could include the following:

- **Technical assistance from experienced consultants:** This is the best form of capacity building. Hands-on support from experienced advisors is likely to be needed to ensure FCs are identified and assessed appropriately in the "first-mover" PPP projects. This provides an opportunity for on-the-job training in which specialists would work with staff members of MoFEP to help assess a proposed PPP project from the FC perspective and thus feed into the FCTC recommendations. Once the transaction is implemented, the consultants can then hand over the analysis (such as source spreadsheets) to the relevant units in MoFEP, along the training needed to monitor and track the FCs during project implementation. This support can be incorporated in the terms of references (TORs) of the TA for these initial projects, or can be performed by expert advisors that would be hired independently to help the FCTC.
- **Formal training courses:** In addition to hands-on training, PID, DMD, and BD officials may benefit from formal training courses. Course selection will depend on individual skills and needs, but could include courses in financial analysis of PPP projects—including risk analysis. Several institutes deliver specific courses on PPPs (such as Right Outcomes, Institute for Public-Private Partnerships (IP3), SMi). If numbers are large enough, courses can be conducted infield and would be tailored to the specific needs of Ghanaian officials.
- **Study tours and secondments:** Study tours or secondments can provide the opportunity for Ghanaian officials to draw directly on the experience of other countries. Staff can get relevant information directly from the source, asking questions and interacting with the main actors involved in the management of FC for PPPs. Partner countries should be carefully chosen to provide the appropriate level of guidance and support to GoG in line with the current state of development of the Ghana PPP program.

Since the proposed approach to evaluating FCs is relatively simple, there should not be any need for specific software—scenario-based analysis of PPP FCs can readily be done in Excel. Going forward, should the GoG adopt more sophisticated analysis, risk assessment "plug-ins" to Excel (such as @Risk or Crystall Ball) would be required.

---

time, MoFEP could consider introducing limits on its overall commitments to PPPs—in coordination with the development of the National Infrastructure Plan (NIP) and the Public Investment Plan (PIP). If the GoG is making repeated use of particular types of commitments or guarantees—such as revenue or exchange rate guarantees—then more sophisticated analytical approaches could be helpful to better analyze the GoG's exposure to the underlying risks, both at the project and portfolio levels. Finally, as Ghana moves toward adopting

International Public Sector Accounting Standards (IPSAS) standards for full accrual accounting, or as further international standards emerge, the approach to reflecting PPP commitments in national accounts may need to be revised to align with international norms.

Finally, the framework set out here is only part of what is needed for responsible management of PPP projects and their associated FCs. This report focuses on the "downstream" aspects of FC management: making sure the costs and fiscal risks arising from GoG support to a PPP are clearly understood and managed responsibly. However, if the underlying project does not make sense, or if the PPP is structured in a way that will not achieve value for money (VfM), then a PPP cannot be fiscally responsible even if its cost is well understood and managed. The PPP Policy sets out guiding principles to that end; it is crucial that the actions set out in this report are complemented by further developing the tools and approaches for choosing and structuring PPP projects well. This should include developing guidance materials and standard approaches for project selection (integrated with the PIP process), VfM analysis, risk allocation, and contract structuring for PPP projects, in line with the discussion in box 6.1.

Notes

1. For instance, the newly approved Petroleum Revenue Management Act (2011) includes disclosure requirements, and a disclosure section has accordingly been added in the Budget Statement. See in pages 28 and 29 of the 2012 Budget Statement: "In accordance with provisions of the Petroleum Revenue Management Act, Act 805, 2011 (PRMA), I now report on the receipts and distribution of oil revenue." For international examples of disclosure requirements for different types of CLs, see Cebotari (2008).

2. Parallel work has supported the GoG in developing a detailed Capacity Building Plan for its PPP program.

REFERENCES AND RELEVANT READINGS

Abrantes, M., P. P. P. de Sousa, and P. T. Lusofonia. 2011. "Managing PPPs for Budget Sustainability: The Case of PPPs in Portugal, from Problems to Solutions." Paper presented at the European Transport Conference 2011. Glasgow, United Kingdom.

Brixi, Hana Polackova. 1998. "Government Contingent Liabilities: A Hidden Risk to Fiscal Stability." Policy Research Working Paper, World Bank.

Brixi, Hana Polackova and Allen Schick. 2002. Government At Risk: Contingent Liabilities and Fiscal Risk. (Oxford: The World Bank and Oxford University Press)

Burger, Philippe, Justin Tyson, Izabela Karpowicz, and Maria Delgado Coelho. 2009. "The Effect of the Financial Crisis on PPPs." IMF Working Paper WP/09/144, International Monetary Fund, Washington, DC.

CEE Bank Watch Network. 2008. Never Mind the Balance Sheet: The Dangers Posed by PPPs in Central and Eastern Europe (CEE).

Clements, B. 2011. "Management of Fiscal Risk from PPPs, presentation in APEC Finance Ministers" presentation in the Process Conference: The Framework and Options for Public Private Financing of Infrastructure.

Clements, B. 2010. The Impact of the Global Financial Crisis on PPPs. Presentation slides, OECD Paris, April 2010.

Cebotari, Aliona. 2008. "Contingent Liabilities: Issues and Practice." IMF Working Paper WP/08/245, International Monetary Fund, Washington, DC.

European Expertise PPP Center—EPEC. 2011. "Risk Distribution and Balance Sheet Treatment: Practical Guide." European Expertise PPP Center—EPEC, Kirchberg, Luxembourg.

European Expertise PPP Center—EPEC. 2011. "State Guarantees in PPPs: A Guide to Better Evaluation, Design, Implementation and Management." European Expertise PPP Center—EPEC, Kirchberg, Luxembourg.

European Expertise PPP Center—EPEC. 2009. "The Financial Crisis and the PPP Market: Potential Remedial Actions." European Expertise PPP Center—EPEC, Kirchberg, Luxembourg.

EIB (European Investment Bank). 2010. "Public and Private Financing for Infrastructure: Evolution and Economics of Private Infrastructure Finance." European Investment Bank, Kirchberg, Luxembourg.

————. 2011a. "National Policy on Public Private Partnership (PPP)." Ministry of Finance and Economic Planning, Government of Ghana.

————. 2011–13. "Medium Term Debt Management Strategy (MTDS)." World Bank, Washington, DC.

————. 2012–14. "Medium Term Deb Management Strategy (MTDS)." World Bank, Washington, DC.

————. 2012. "Draft PPP Law Interim Report." March-April. Unpublished manuscript.

Government of Chile. 2011. "Informe de Pasivos Contingentes 2011 (Contingent Liabilities Report, in Spanish)." http://www.dipres.gob.cl/572/articles-76644_IPC_2011.pdf.

Government of Ghana. 2012. "The Budget Statement and Economic Policy of the Government of Ghana for 2012 Fiscal Year." Presented to Parliament November 16, 2011 by Dr. Kwabena Duffuor, Minister o Finance and Economic Planning.

————. 2011. National Policy on Public-Private Partnerships.

————. 2009. Annual Accounts and Controller and Accountant General (CAG) Report.

————. Medium Term Debt Management Strategy (MTDS), 2012–2014.

————. Medium Term Debt Management Strategy (MTDS), 2011–2013.

Hemming, R., and Staff Team. 2006. *PPPs Government Guarantees, and Fiscal Risk.* Washington, DC: IMF Publication.

India Planning Commission. 2010. "Report of the Task Force on Ceilings for Annuity Commitments."

IMF (International Monetary Fund). 2001. *Government Finance Statistics Manual.* Washington, DC: IMF.

Irwin, T. 2003. "Public Money for Private Infrastructure: Deciding When to Offer Guarantees, Output-Based Subsidies, and Other Fiscal Support," World Bank Working Paper No. 10, World Bank, Washington, DC.

————. 2007. *Government Guarantees: Allocating and Valuing Risk in Privately Financed Infrastructure Projects.*" Washington, DC: World Bank publication.

Irwin, T., and T. Mokdad. 2009. *Managing Contingent Liabilities in PPPs: Practice in Australia, Chile, and South Africa.* Washington, DC: World Bank and PPIAF Publication.

Kim, J. 2008. "Fiscal Risk Management in PPPs." Presentation at the 3rd Annual Meeting on PPP Promotion between Japan and Korea.

Monteiro, Rui. 2007. "PPP and Fiscal Risks: Experiences from Portugal", presentation slides in Internal Seminar on Strengthening Public Investment and Managing Fiscal Risks form PPPs. Hungary, March 2007.

————. 2011. The Impact of Fiscal Treatment of PPPs on their Efficiency and Integrity: The Case of Eurostat Rules, presentation slides, World Bank September 2011.

Partnership Victoria, "Part One: Partnership Victoria Risk Allocation Principles"

Villafuerte et al. 2009. Namibia: PPPs: Building A Framework for Managing Fiscal Risks. IMF Publication.

Wells, L. T., and R. Ahmed. 2006. *Making Foreign Investment Safe: Property Rights and National Sovereignty.* Oxford: Oxford University Press.

World Bank. 2010. "Africa Infrastructure Country Diagnostic." Ghana Country Report AICD, Washington, DC.

World Bank and Castalia. 2011. "Support for the Implementation of a Fiscal Commitment and Contingent Liability management Framework for PPPs in Nigeria." Unpublished manuscript.

WBI (World Bank Institute). 2012. *PPP Reference Guide Version 1.0.* Washington, DC: World Bank.

Short-Term Action Plan
for GoG to Manage FCs from PPPs

This report outlines an approach for Government of Ghana (GoG) to manage its fiscal commitments (FCs) from public-private partnerships (PPPs) to ensure that those commitments are well understood and assessed before the PPP project is approved, and that they are monitored, reported on, and budgeted for over the lifetime of the PPP contracts. The report outlines processes, roles, and responsibilities for undertaking these functions. Most of the recommendations in this report can be immediately applied at the same time as the "first mover" projects of the PPP program are developed and implemented. Others are points to consider as the PPP program expands or when Ghana adopts updated accounting standards (such as accrual or International Public Sector Accounting Standards [IPSAS]).

In light of the recommendations presented in the report, appendix A provides a short summary of decisions and actions that the GoG can make in the short term to make immediate progress toward implementing a sound management framework for PPP FCs. For each decision or activity outlined below, further details and rationales are provided in the main text of this report (see table A.1).

Table A.1 List of Activities and Responsible Parties for a PPP FC Framework

Topic	Responsible agency	Activity/decision
Institutional roles and responsibilities	PID (PFA and SOE units), DMD, BD, ERFD	• Agree on the roles of DMD, ERFD, BD, and PID (PFA and SOE units • Identify specific staff in each of these divisions to be responsible for this agenda. These staff members will work closely with PPP project Transaction Advisors on FC-related matters. • Establish a FCTC with a clear mandate to manage FCs from PPP projects.

(table continues on next page)

Table A.1 List of Activities and Responsible Parties for a PPP FC Framework (continued)

Topic	Responsible agency	Activity/decision
Legislative requirements to feed into the proposed PPP Law	PID and PPP Approval Committee	Chapter 4 highlights some key FC issues that can be addressed in the PPP Law currently being drafted. The proposed input relates to (1) information sharing by the concessionaire to enable assessing and monitoring FC; (2) assigning responsibilities for assessing, monitoring, and reporting FC from PPPs; (3) clarifying approval processes for PPP projects that receive guarantees and government in-kind support; and (4) disclosing PPP contract information.
TORs for Feasibility Studies and Transaction Advisory (TA) work	PAU	PAU to provide guidance on TORs for the procurement of Feasibility Studies/Transaction Advisory consultants, and to ensure that FC information and analysis requirements are adequately addressed. TORs for first-mover projects should also include on-the-job training provided by the consultants for FCTC members on interpreting this information and assessing affordability.
Budgeting approach for direct and contingent PPP liabilities	Budget Division and DMD	As first-mover projects are developed and implemented, define the approach to budgeting for direct and contingent PPP liabilities, including the following: • Confirming the budget approach for direct PPP FCs, including whether these payments will be made through MDAs or from a central account • Agreeing on the approach to setting the level of the CL contingency budget for different types of CLs • Undertaking necessary incorporations in the Ghana Integrated Financial Management Information System (GIFMIS) program, currently being developed, to reflect GoG decisions on how to reflect PPP FC in the government budget.
Stocktaking and reporting on FCs from PPPs	PAU, BD, DMD	• Collate information on FCs under existing PPP contracts (see table A.2). • Disclose in forthcoming government reports (MTDS, Budget Statement, notes to National Accounts) information on FCs to PPPs (existing projects, and first mover projects as they are signed), including a description of the nature of the project and commitment, and an estimate of its value where possible (annual cost and NPV for direct commitments; at least the maximum cost for CLs) • As necessary, discuss with the IMF the appropriate approach to recognizing PPP liabilities in debt measures for first mover PPP types • Develop template PPP project contract briefs, summarizing the key elements of PPP contracts and procurement processes, and publish these briefs on PID website for first-mover PPP contracts.
SOE management and its integration with PPP FC management	DMD and PID SOE Unit	• Clearly assign the unit/division to be responsible for monitoring the financial positions and governance of SOEs entering in PPP projects (this is currently divided between the SOE Unit in PID and the Domestic Debt Unit in DMD).
Approving a FC framework for GoG	PID and PPP Approval Committee	• Synthesize the recommendations in this report in a government-owned document on the FC framework to be adopted for the PPP program.

Source: World Bank data.

Note: BD = Budget Division; CLs = contingent liabilities; DMD = Debt Management Division; ERFD = Economic Research and Forecasting Division; FC = fiscal commitments; FCTC = Fiscal Commitment Technical Committee; GoG = Government of Ghana; IMF = International Monetary Fund; MDAs = Ministries, Departments and Agencies; MTDS = Medium Term Debt Strategy; NPV = net present value; PAU = Project Advisory Unit; PFA = Project and Financial Analysis Unit; PID = Public Investment Division; PPP = public-private partnership; SOE = State-Owned Enterprise; TORs = terms of references.

Table A.2 Proposed PPP Projects for Stocktaking FC

Project	Sector	Status of project (to be confirmed by GoG)
Meridian Port Services- MPS Tema Terminal Concession	Port	Signed in 2002/03
Tema Osonor Power Plant	Power	Signed/Almost Signed
Cen Power (signed ECG)	Power	Signed/Almost Signed
Asogle Power Plant (signed VRA)	Power	Signed/Almost Signed
Teshie-Nungua desalination project.	Water	Signed 2012
Asutsuare Treatment Plant	Water	Negotiations in progress
Accra-Kumasi Dualization	Roads	Negotiations in progress
Accra-Tema Dualization	Roads	Negotiations in progress
Expatriate Identity Card PPP Project	Other	In progress

Source: World Bank data.

Note: GoG = Government of Ghana; ECG = Electricity Company of Ghana; PPP = public-private partnership; VRA = Volta River Author

FC Reporting and Disclosure Templates

This report highlights the importance of reporting on fiscal commitments (FCs) under public-private partnership (PPP) projects, both internally and publicly. Appendix B provides simple templates that could be used to present this information: in notes to the annual accounts; in budget statements; and as part of debt sustainability reporting.

Long-Term Expenditure Commitments

Table B.1 provides information on long-term Government of Ghana (GoG) expenditure commitments under PPP contracts. Discussion in text should describe key risks or exposures at the overall portfolio level.

Table B.1 Long-Term Expenditure Commitments to Public-Private Partnerships

PPP project	Description of commitment	Annual payment value for the 3 budget years (GHC million)				Estimated present value of all future obligations (GHC million)
		Current year	Budget year	MTEF Y 2	MTEF Y 3	As of current year
Toll Road A	Shadow toll paid annually;	#	#	#	#	#
	Duration X years;					
	Denominated in [or indexed to] Y currency					
Toll Road B						
Toll Road C						
Total (Transport)						
Prison A	Annual availability payment;	#	#	#	#	#
	Duration X years;					
	Denominated in Y currency					
Hospital A						
Total (Other)						
Total						

Source: World Bank data.
Note: GHC = Ghanaian Cedi; MTEF = Medium Term Expenditure Framework; PPP = public-private partnership.

Contingent Liabilities

Contingent Liabilities (CLs) are obligations whose occurrence, timing, and magnitude depend on the occurrence of some uncertain future event. The source(s) of CLs to government reported below [are/include] the government's commitments under PPP contracts. Discussion in text should describe key risks or exposures at the overall portfolio level (see table B.2). *[This note could be expanded in future to cover other types of CLs beyond those associated with PPPs.]*

Table B.2 CLs under PPPs

PPP project	Description of project	Description of contingent liabilities	Actual payments (GHC million)	Estimated payments over MTEF period[a] (GHC million)			Estimated present value of all future obligations (GHC million)
			Current FY	Budget year	MTEF Y2	MTEF Y3	As of current year
Toll road A	100 km toll road linking A to B; 25 year contract dated 201X; Operational from 201Y	• Government bears two *ongoing* CLs:	#	#	#	#	#
		• Minimum Revenue Guarantee	#	#	#	#	#
		• Exchange Rate Guarantee					
		• In case of contract termination government has a *one-off payment commitment* of a value between GHC X and Y million, depending on cause of termination.					
Toll road B							
Toll road C							
Total (Transport)							
Prison A							
Hospital A							
Total (Other)							
Total							

Source: World Bank data.

Note: GHC = Ghanaian Cedi; MTEF = Medium Term Expenditure Framework; PPP = public-private partnership.

a. Estimates calculated from "base case" scenario assumptions. Other "down sound" scenarios should also be considered and reported internally.